JUST STAND

WHAT TO DO
WHEN YOU WANT TO GIVE UP

KRIS VALLOTTON

WHITAKER
HOUSE

JUST STAND:
What to Do When You Want to Give Up

Kris Vallotton
www.krisvallotton.com
info@kvministries.com

ISBN: 979-8-88769-443-6
eBook ISBN: 979-8-88769-444-3

Printed in the United States of America
© 2025 by Kris Vallotton

Whitaker House
1030 Hunt Valley Circle
New Kensington, PA 15068
www.whitakerhouse.com

Library of Congress Cataloging-in-Publication Data

Names: Vallotton, Kris author
Title: Just stand : what to do when you want to give up / Kris Vallotton.
Identifiers: LCCN 2025021937 (print) | LCCN 2025021938 (ebook) | ISBN
  9798887694436 hardcover | ISBN 9798887694443 ebook
Subjects: LCSH: Self-actualization (Psychology)--Religious
  aspects--Christianity | Asthenia--Religious aspects--Christianity |
  Spiritual life--Christianity | BISAC: RELIGION / Christian Living /
  Spiritual Growth | RELIGION / Christian Living / Personal Growth
Classification: LCC BV4598.2 .V345 2025 (print) | LCC BV4598.2 (ebook) |
  DDC 248.8/6--dc23/eng/20250710
LC record available at https://lccn.loc.gov/2025021937
LC ebook record available at https://lccn.loc.gov/2025021938

1 2 3 4 5 6 7 8 9 10 11   31 30 29 28 27 26 25

DEDICATION

I dedicate this book to all of you who, like me, have found yourselves in a storm that threatens to derail your faith, challenge your sanity, and/or be more than you can handle alone. My prayer and purposeful intention in writing this manuscript is that it would be a lifeline—giving you hope and a lighthouse to guide you through the tempest of the dark night of the soul to the safe harbor of peace.

CONTENTS

ACKNOWLEDGMENT

I want to thank Don Milam, who, long ago, worked for Destiny Image Publishing, my first publisher. Don was the company's acquisitions person when I first met him. At the time, no one was interested in publishing a book by me because I was unknown and had never written anything before. Don met with me as a favor to Bill Johnson and was gracious enough to let me read two chapters of my first manuscript to him as he listened intently. When I finished reading, he looked at me and said, "You're an incredible writer! We'll publish anything you write." Don's belief in me changed my life.

Don Milam went home to be with the Lord this year, and so many of us authors who were discovered by this amazing man owe him a huge debt of gratitude. We love you, Don, and we will meet you again in eternity!

INTRODUCTION: "AND HAVING DONE EVERYTHING..."

MY JOURNEY TO STANDING STRONG

The world is full of talented, gifted, intelligent people, many of whom love God and have so much potential, yet they are often derailed by their circumstances, undermined by their failures, or paralyzed by their poor choices. They spend much of their life living past-present, allowing their history to become their destiny. I was one of those people! I had an incredibly rough upbringing, losing my dad when I was three years young and growing up with a ton of pain. I married my childhood sweetheart, Kathy, when I was twenty years old. Just two years later, I had a severe nervous breakdown that lasted for more than three years. (I'll share more of my journey with you in the coming chapters.)

Then, after twenty years of running nine businesses, Kathy and I left the business world in 1998 and joined the ministry team at Bethel Church in Redding, California. In the midst of incredible growth, both personally and in ministry—including thousands of miracles, deliverances, and salvations—there have also been extremely difficult seasons of warfare, disappointment, and suffering. In fact, the warfare became so intense in my personal life that, in 2008, I had a second nervous breakdown that nearly ended my life. It took me a year and a half to recover. From that time on, I determined that, no matter how much I might feel like giving up, I would learn how to stand firm and live in peace in the midst of the storms of life. Jesus is our model, and He slept in a boat in the midst of a horrible storm while His disciples, several of whom were fishermen, panicked in fear for their lives. I reasoned that if Jesus could stand in perfect peace in the storms of life, then His example must be an invitation for us to experience the same sense of peace in our tempestuous conditions and circumstances.

My life has changed drastically since 2008. I have learned to weather some extremely turbulent times with an extraordinary level of peace in my soul—sometimes to my own amazement and always with gratitude. Consequently, thousands of people who are looking for peace and strength have been drawn to my story and have benefited from hearing what I learned: not just how to avoid storms but how to stand strong in the midst of them.

A DIVINE INVITATION

The apostle Paul knew a thing or two about storms. Chained to the wall of a cold, dark prison beneath the ground in the Greek city of Ephesus, he wrote, "*Therefore, take up the full armor of God, so that you will be able to resist in the evil day, and **having done everything, to stand firm**. Stand firm therefore...*" (Ephesians 6:13–14). The truth is, we often have no control over the weather of our lives, but we can learn to prepare for the storms, find shelter in the Lord, and stay standing while those storms rage around us.

Hundreds of books have been written on the subject of peace, and I'm sure many of them are very good. Yet this book is more like an invitation to join me on my journey to stand strong in contentedness and confidence than it is an intellectual jousting of philosophies on the psychology of peace. I want to help clothe you in armor and prepare you for those dark times and stormy circumstances that tend to suck you into the clutches of hopelessness and despair.

Whether you are struggling to find peace in a tough situation, or you've lived a turbulent life of anxiety, fear, and/or anguish, this book is for you! I pray that the words penned in this book become a lighthouse glistening in the night, showing you the way through the raging waters of life's vulnerabilities and guiding you into the safe harbor of security and tranquility.

Peace be to you and all that matters to you! I'll meet you again in chapter 1....

1

"GIVE ME YOUR ASHES"

Life is like setting sail on a great sea of adventure. While some people are fortunate enough to inherit a grand cruise ship to begin their journey, others are born on a life raft or maybe even a floating branch, left to navigate the harsh reality of the ocean with a seemingly slim chance of survival. Yet with whatever vessel we are launched, no one—no matter what their privileged condition—can avoid the storms of life and the uncertainties of the sea of human existence. No silver spoon, large bank account, Beverly Hills mansion, or even healthy family can isolate you from troubles, trials, and suffering; they're just part of life on this side of heaven. Yet, the truth is, God has not only equipped us all for the voyage, but He's also called us to *stand* to plant our feet in faith when everything around us is shifting, and to remain steady when the waves rise. He doesn't just want to keep us afloat; He wants to teach us how to still storms, walk on water, and stand firm when everything in us wants to collapse.

THE "LAST SUPPER"

Standing isn't always easy! In fact, it was especially hard for me to stand during a crisis period in my life several years ago. On October 31, 2022, I took Kathy, my wife, to dinner. We sat across the table from each other as we had done so many times before, but this meal was different: this was my "last supper." I sat there for a long time just staring at her as I tried to gain my composure. Finally, through my tears, I eked out, "I am tired, and my time at Bethel Church feels like it's over! I want to resign and move on with my life." I cupped my hands and gestured as if I were letting something fly away. Kathy sat there with a reassuring look on her face. When I paused, she reached across the table and took my hand. "I understand," she said in a compassionate tone. "You've been through a lot," she went on to say, squeezing my hand while looking directly into my eyes, "and you've tried your best to make it all work." I continued to pour out my broken heart to her for a while as she listened intently.

After we returned home, I went up to our room, threw myself on our bed, and sobbed. I had worked for Bethel for twenty-four long, hard, and extremely fruitful years. But now I was mentally, emotionally, and spiritually exhausted. The thought of continuing there made me sick to my stomach. I was discouraged, and I felt unappreciated and misunderstood. Furthermore, the road ahead was steep, and it was riddled with tough decisions that had to be made. They were the kind of decisions in which nobody wins, the "lesser of two evils" kind of stuff. I was in the driver's seat; it was my call, but the way forward was unclear—painful at best and disastrous at worst. Money was extremely tight, our team wasn't on the same page, and our senior leader had recently lost his wife to cancer. The mood was somber, serious, and cautious. The times demanded a strong, faith-filled leader who had a vision and wasn't dragging around a sack filled with the dry bones of failed ventures. I cried myself to sleep that night.

Then, at about three in the morning, I had a powerful dream. In this dream, a bird—a cardinal—was in my hands, and I was trying desperately to get it to fly away. Opening my hands, I shouted, "Go...fly...get out of here!" but nothing worked. Finally, I grabbed the bird and threw it into the air. It flew around my head several times and then landed on my shoulder. Then, suddenly, a voice in the dream proclaimed, "You can't give away what I have given you! Now, give Me your ashes!" I woke up to hear this proclamation from Isaiah the prophet ringing in my spirit: "I'm going to give them 'beauty for ashes, the oil of joy for mourning.'" (See Isaiah 61:3 NKJV.)

I lay there for what seemed like an eternity contemplating the Lord's salutation and staring at my ash heap in my mind. In one way, I felt reassured that the Lord acknowledged that I had been through a gauntlet of painful circumstances that had climaxed in a heap of ashes. I felt His compassion for my situation, and I knew that I was understood, seen, and known by Him. At the same time, I struggled with dying to myself and my need to find an off-ramp from the intense anguish I was experiencing in the role I was playing. I couldn't see a painless way forward; thus, I wrestled with hopelessness and despair.

I WOKE UP TO HEAR THIS PROCLAMATION FROM ISAIAH THE PROPHET RINGING IN MY SPIRIT: "I'M GOING TO GIVE THEM 'BEAUTY FOR ASHES, THE OIL OF JOY FOR MOURNING.'"

That night, I remembered a counseling appointment I'd had years ago with a mom of three small children who had lost her husband in a car accident a couple of years earlier. She was fighting off depression, which was uncommon for her. As she sat in my office and unpacked her story, I saw the problem clearly, and I said, "You never grieved the loss of your husband because you needed to be strong for your children. You've had to bring stability to your kids, so you haven't had time to mourn. Yet Jesus said, 'Blessed are those who mourn, for they shall be comforted' (Matthew 5:4). It's time for you to mourn so you can find comfort." She began sobbing uncontrollably, and she wept for more than an hour as I reassured her of God's grace to restore her and her children. Several years later, she married a prince of a man who adopted her children and became an incredible father to them.

When I recalled this counseling session, I was surprised to realize that I was like that woman. Over the past couple of years, many of the church's dreams had seemed to die, and I had needed to be strong for our congregation and our team; therefore, I'd had no time to grieve over those losses. In fact, I had been trying so hard to stay positive, to be encouraging, and to live future-present that I had sort of convinced myself that there was nothing to mourn—there was no ash heap; it was all a mirage! The truth is, we had been to hell and back, and we were fortunate to still be alive!

I awoke the next morning feeling hopeful for the first time in a couple of years. Over the next few weeks, the Lord began to reveal a plan for us to rise from the ash heap. Eventually, like the mythical phoenix, we emerged from the fire of affliction stronger and healthier than ever. (I'll describe more about this process as we go along.) Was it hard? Heck yeah! But it has been incredibly rewarding!

How about you: Do you have an ash heap? Maybe, like me, the responsibilities of life and the need to be strong for others has kept you in a state of denial, yet your lack of closure for these things keeps raising its ugly head, often at the most inconvenient times. Well, I want to reassure you that God is the Master of bringing beauty out of ashes. He doesn't create beauty out of nothing!

"JUST STANDING" ISN'T PASSIVE

There are so many people walking around in incredible amounts of pain—none of us is exempt from it. The mission of this book is to give your pain a purpose and to encourage you that you are going to be okay. In chapter 2, we will delve deeper into the reality that, often, the darkest seasons of our lives are cocoons—environments that give birth to a radical transformation in and through us. This book is about learning to stand when you want to give up. It's about finding the grace to stay grounded when the winds of life try to blow you over. Inside these pages, you'll discover practical wisdom for navigating these epoch seasons with grace so that the darkness does not overtake you, and you come through standing stronger than ever.

STANDING IS WHAT HAPPENS WHEN YOUR WEAKNESS COLLIDES WITH GOD'S STRENGTH.

"Just standing" doesn't mean gritting your teeth, striving harder, or pulling yourself up by your own bootstraps (although, in fairness, there still may be some days like that). It means anchoring your heart in the strength of God and understanding that He's not finished writing your story. Let me be clear: standing isn't passive. It's powerful. It's what happens when your weakness collides with His strength. The God of mercy and grace is inviting you to the place where His power shows up in your pressure and where your inability becomes the backdrop for His supernatural ability. This is how we stand strong—not in ourselves, but in Him.

A WORD FOR THE WEARY

Those who are perishing in the midst of their pain will find the hope to endure in every chapter of this book. *Just Stand* is more than survival tips; it's a roadmap for transformation. We'll explore what it means to undergo true metamorphosis instead of just moving through another transition. We'll see how to let go of the weights that are holding us back, build life-giving ecosystems that support real change, and discover God's purposes working in the most challenging times. We'll talk about failing forward, what it looks like to get back up after disobedience, and how to walk wisely with prophetic words so they actually come to pass. We'll expose common pitfalls, confront temptation, and dive into what it means to courageously stand strong—not just for our own break-throughs but as a light in a world that desperately needs hope.

I don't know where you are in your journey in life or in your relationship with the Lord. But I want to both challenge you and reassure you. First, let me challenge you: my life is full of tough times, but God is the One who has caused bad things, hard things, painful things, *everything* to somehow work out in my favor for me, for those in my family, and for my church. It's not magic—it's Jesus. And although I have made a lot of mistakes, screwed many things up, done it wrong, said it wrong, bought it wrong…the one thing I have never done wrong is to follow Him. There is a prerequisite for prospering in every circumstance, and it is that we love Him.

Jesus put it best: *"If you love Me, you will keep My commandments. I will ask the Father, and He will give you another Helper, that He may be with you forever"* (John 14:15–16). What does it look like to love Christ? Jesus said, *"You will keep my commandments."* We live in a world of relative righteousness; nobility has become a relic of religion, deemed out of style and outdated, uncool—not in step with twenty-first-century hipsters. William Booth, the founder of the Salvation Army, wrote, "The chief dangers which confront the coming century will be religion without the Holy Ghost; Christianity without Christ; forgiveness without repentance; salvation without regeneration; politics without God; and Heaven without Hell."[1] Well, William certainly got that one right!

Nevertheless, the Scripture emphatically states that everything in life works out for good *"to those who* **love God**, *to those who are* **called** *according to* **His** *purpose"* (Romans 8:28). This book is about loving God practically and walking in His purposes so we can see His sovereign hand at work in our lives, *"making all things new"* (Revelation 21:5)! It's time to enjoy the journey.

---

1. William Booth, in "Dangers of the Century," *War Cry* [Salvation Army newspaper], January 5, 1901, 7. Originally published in *The New York World*, December 30, 1900.

2

IT'S DARK IN HERE: METAMORPHOSIS

They say that great people rise in dark times; I think that's true. But I don't think it's necessarily because they have stronger personalities or are dramatically more gifted than the average person (although some are). I think it's most often because they view life with a different lens, and they relate to their circumstances with a sort of "sixth sense." This gives them a sense of hope in which they anticipate a positive outcome and position themselves for increase and/or blessing. History testifies to us that adversity is often the mother of invention, innovation, and creativity. Of course, adversity is also the father of disaster, destruction, and failure. So, hard times don't always build great people, reveal better opportunities, or cause positive outcomes, but they certainly can. I mean, "live and learn" is not a given. Many people live out their lives never learning from their mistakes.

I have been through a lot of adversity that I've navigated well at times and not so well during other seasons of my life. But I don't think I have ever experienced the frequency of challenges that my local community, my church, and I personally have faced over the last six years. Have you ever lived a nightmare that you feared you'd never wake up from? I certainly have, and one thing I have learned through these tough years is that what the devil calls buried, God calls planted!

WHAT THE DEVIL CALLS BURIED, GOD CALLS PLANTED!

THE CARR FIRE

Let me tell you a few of the highlights (or should I say *lowlights*) of our story. For me, the intense challenges began with the Carr Fire (one of the largest fires in California history) that tore through our city and ravaged our community, killing eight people. It looked like a scene out of an apocalypse movie: the sky dark with smoke and ash falling all over our city. These conditions continued for months on end. In the midst of this darkness, Bethel Church became a distribution center for the Salvation Army, and our staff and congregation volunteered for weeks to get the most-needed essentials to our community. Our Bethel Global Response Teams (BGR) worked around the clock to provide relief for the displaced victims of the fire. Our teams, dressed in hazmat suits in 100-degree weather, sifted through heaps of ashes looking for some beauty in the burned remnants. We went on to raise $1.5 million in two days to help fund the people who'd been displaced by the fire, giving each of them a thousand dollars, no matter their religious convictions. A few months later, we raised another seven hundred thousand dollars to buy equipment and to fund teams to help rebuild our city. We commissioned the BGR teams and sent them into the devastated neighborhoods to clear the burned trees from individual properties so that our neighbors could begin to rebuild their homes. This process took nearly two years of hard, dirty labor. Our main objective was to restore hope to our community.

THE PANDEMIC

Just as the air began to clear and the residents of Redding were gaining momentum in the restoration of our broken city, disaster struck again. It was on January 20, 2020, that the first case of COVID-19 was discovered in America. By March of the same year, the governor of California had ordered all the churches and schools in the state to close. The timing couldn't have been worse because it was just two months before we were to graduate twenty-six hundred Bethel School of Supernatural Ministry students who had come to Redding from seventy-two nations. And, as if that weren't hard enough, we were given a week's notice to move all our students from our physical campus to an online learning platform (which we didn't have)! Our Bethel teams scrambled to scrape together a makeshift plan, working literally around the clock. The following week, we began streaming our services to our congregation, with fifty of our staff members in a sanctuary that held nine hundred people. The same week, our school teams moved all our classes to a temporary online learning platform that we managed to launch on Monday. (In a later chapter, I describe the all-out effort it took for us to put together a complete online ministry school for the fall semester—and what it means to suffer with others during difficult times and form deep bonds as we share in that experience.) A couple of months later, we held a "drive-through graduation," handing each of our students their diplomas as they drove through our parking lot. I bet you have your own world-turned-upside-down COVID-19 stories as well.

THE FLOYD FACTOR

In the midst of our trying to recover from the whirlwind of a disastrous couple of months, with our staff literally finishing the school year running on fumes (between navigating a disgruntled congregation, student population, and city), George Floyd was killed by a police officer on May 25 of the same year. Several of our Black staff members were thrust into a deep depression as they struggled to comprehend their own plight. Many of them feared for their lives and couldn't even leave their homes! This triggered reactions of accusation from some of our Black staff members and students, where they felt Bethel Church and its staff were racist. By June, some of our senior leaders and I were proactively engaged in agonizing, passionate group discussions with them. We struggled to understand the depth of their pain as, apparently, we were a part of the problem! I had never before been accused of being racist. My father's best friend was Black; they grew up playing football together. When my father drowned, his friend brought our family into his own home and took care of us. Furthermore, growing up, I attended a racially integrated high school where many of my closest friends were African American. Heck, for that matter, I was the only white kid in the Black History class. Later in my life, I was part of the team at Bethel when our church planted twelve ministry schools in Africa and poured millions of dollars into helping to care for the continent.

But the painful truth is, although we were far from racist, it became very apparent that our primarily white Republican city and church certainly had a lot to learn about Black culture. I left most of those group discussions in tears as our Black staff members and students described the trauma caused by our ignorance. For example, they pointed out that Donald Trump's campaign slogan "Make America Great Again" insinuates that there was a time when America was "greater," and that we needed to get "back" to this better time. Yet, for African Americans, the past is filled with pain caused by slavery, bigotry, prejudice, discrimination, lynchings, and whippings. No Black person thinks the United States was better off previously than it is today, especially after the nation elected its first Black president! I could write an entire book on the painful process of those meetings—what we learned and how we are endeavoring to make adjustments. But it will suffice to say here that maturing, for all of us, is often an agonizing process. I want to remind you that not all pain is bad. For example, it's impossible to grow your physical body without experiencing some muscle pain. In the same way, the discomfort of life's circumstances is often what is producing a greater glory in each of us!

THE SHAME CAMPAIGN

By September 2020, COVID-19 was spreading like wildfire! Five hundred of our students and staff became infected over a three-month period; our local hospitals were full, and our city was in a panic. We operated with a skeleton crew for months as our staff members became sick or rotated in and out of quarantine. Despite our wearing masks, social distancing, scrubbing ourselves down like we were preparing for surgery, and working mostly from home, there seemed to be no relief in sight. Ultimately, I caught the virus and became really sick. I was in bed for nine days and had intense symptoms for six weeks. But on October 17, 2020, I dragged myself out of bed and performed my grandson Elijah's outdoor wedding, which we moved to our small farm in the mountains in Shingletown, California, reducing the guest list from three hundred to a hundred and twenty people. As a result, from October 19–26, I was repeatedly mentioned in the press for having performed an outdoor wedding during COVID. (By the way, it was legal for restaurants to serve people outdoors at the time.) I just couldn't catch a break.

A couple of weeks later, the director of the Shasta County Health Department testified before the Shasta County Board of Supervisors that Bethel School of Ministry was responsible for the COVID-19 virus in our city, which was absolutely not true! The director apologized to me the next day and admitted that he was wrong, although there was no public apology. Consequently, many of our students were fired from their jobs, and several weren't even allowed to use the laundry rooms in their apartment complexes. On top of that, there was continuous negative press, and it felt like we were being publicly shamed. It's downright crazy when bad things happen to good people through no fault of their own. I felt so bad for our students—but welcome to the WORLD!

These circumstances felt like a page right out of the book of Acts, where Paul and Barnabas healed a lame man in the city of Lystra and were at first celebrated as gods. But, the next day, some people who opposed them came to the city and convinced the community to stone them as heretics! (See Acts 14:8–23.) One day you're doing fine, and the next day you're doing time! Of course, I am joking, but what is true is that crowds are fickle. Anybody on social media? *Case closed.*

I CAN TRUMP THAT

Just when I was about to ask myself what else could go wrong, the presidential election reached its climactic outcome. I had accurately prophesied both of George W. Bush's presidential terms, both of Barack Obama's presidential terms, and Donald Trump's first presidential term. Unfortunately, in December 2019, I shared a word about divine providence with the Bethel congregation, and, at the end of my message, I confidently pronounced from the podium on a Sunday morning that Donald Trump would win the next presidential election. But, on November 7, 2020, Joe Biden won the US presidency, and, of course, Donald Trump lost! Although I had ministered in the governmental realm for nearly two decades and had never before missed a political prophecy in all those years (that I am aware of), this was devastating to me, to say the least. On November 9, I publicly apologized for the inaccurate prophetic word I had given concerning Donald Trump's second term. Then *all hell broke loose!* Have you ever felt like you would just like to run away where no one could find you and never come back?

This situation rightly created a credibility gap for my ministry, for which I take full responsibility. It was especially tough for the people who had trusted my ministry and maybe even voted for Donald Trump because of my prophetic word. Understandably, those folks were disappointed in me, and many of them reached out to let me know that they were no longer following my ministry. Then there were an equal number of people who were very angry that I had apologized for my inaccurate prophetic word, believing that I had betrayed God by not contending for the word to *miraculously* come to pass. Many of them were convinced that Donald Trump was in fact the president of the United States, and they refused to acknowledge Joe Biden as our newly elected leader. Others shouted, "The election was stolen by the corrupt left," and some even advocated a civil war! You can imagine the hate mail I received when I congratulated Joe Biden and Kamala Harris on their victory and welcomed them as our president and vice president in my letter of apology, committing to pray for them.

TIME TO LEAVE

As you might imagine, with eight hundred staff members from twenty or so countries and a very strong, diverse senior team, there was a lot of debate among us about how to handle all these situations. After all, none of us had ever before navigated a global pandemic, much less all the other circumstances that piled on top of us day after day. The negative financial side effects of all these situations were also growing, adding up to multiple millions of dollars. Between canceling twenty-eight of our events two years in a row, our on-campus school of ministry attendance dropping by a thousand students, our media company sales reduced by five million dollars, and our congregation moving to an online platform for the better part of a year, things in the natural were looking incredibly bleak! But our challenges weren't nearly over yet.

In January 2021, Eric and Candace Johnson, who had been the senior pastors of our local church for ten years, decided to leave to plant a church in Greenville, North Carolina. I was shocked, and Bill Johnson (Eric's father and our senior leader) was devastated! We all thought they would stay at Bethel forever, especially since they were doing such a great job building community among our congregation. However, this is what they felt God was calling them to do, and we sent them off with our blessing. But, predictively, many of their team announced that they were going with them to plant the church. Personally, I struggled with the thought of trying to navigate the exodus of so many of our key leaders at such a crucial and critical time in our history. This was becoming a wild and treacherous ride with no end in sight, but the worst was yet to come! Have you ever been there?

CONTENDING FOR HEALING

The week that Eric and Candace were leaving for good to plant their church in Greenville, Beni Johnson, Bill's wife, was diagnosed with stage 4 cancer. Our Bethel congregation contended for her healing for more than a year. While many others in our ministry were getting healed of the same disease, it wasn't to be for Beni. Eighteen months later, on July 13, 2022, Beni Johnson passed away! Have you ever experienced grief and sadness at this level yourself?

MEANWHILE, BACK AT THE RANCH

It's hard to describe what it's like to live in an era of so much chaos and confusion. Words could never do it justice. One of the greatest challenges we were facing during the COVID-19 season was uncertainty, which created a ton of fear in all of us. The truth is that certainty rooted in circumstances is actually fantasy; it's not reality. Yet the illusion that we are in control of our future, and therefore that life is predictable, brings us a lot of peace. The opposite is true when the circumstances of everyday life change continually, without notice, and especially when you're facing things you have never experienced before.

Yet there is a certainty found in the person of Jesus, an assurance rooted in the nature of a good God who cares for us and, as we discussed in chapter 1, causes all things (good things, bad things, everything) to work out in our favor when we trust and serve Him. I've believed this truth in my head for decades, but much like the foundational pylons underneath skyscrapers that have been pounded into the ground to support the height and weight of those huge buildings, the intensity of the hour was pounding this truth deep into our souls.

For me, this profound pounding started when I was sick with the COVID virus, as I relayed earlier. In bed for nine long days, and so weak that I could barely walk to the bathroom, I honestly thought I might die. On my seventh day in bed, the Lord spoke to me at about five in the morning, saying, *You must get out of this bed and lead My people!* I responded out loud, "I can't even get out of bed. How am I going to lead anyone?" There was no reply. Have you ever had the Lord give you an assignment in which you had *no* capacity to succeed? The next morning, He spoke to me again: *You must get out of this bed and lead My people!* Despite the urgency in His voice, it had no effect on my body; I was still so weak that I could barely sit up. Can you relate?

But the following morning, I managed to get out of bed, even though I was shaky and frail. Then, as my feet touched the floor, I felt something supernatural take place inside my soul. It was as if I were Rocky Balboa, knocked down in the boxing ring, with the referee standing over his lifeless body, counting him out: one, two, three, four, five, six, seven…. Suddenly, Rocky grabs the rope and pulls himself to his feet, staggering to his corner while motioning to his opponent to bring it on. The crowd stands to its feet, chanting his name, as the theme song from Rocky ensues. I know…I know…a little melodramatic, but the feeling was real in me. I knew that the Lord had instilled a new strength in me and that it was time to *just stand*.

A TIME TO UNITE

A couple of weeks later, I gathered together about seventy of our most prominent Bethel leaders to inspire a new resolve and to build a strategy to get us off the proverbial mat. I honestly had no idea what I was going to say, but there was a righteous anger burning in my spirit that needed an outlet. I began with the first few scripted lines of my exhortation: "We are going through a massive—" I was about to say, "a massive transition," but before I could squeak out the word *transition*, the Lord interrupted my thoughts. He said, *You are not going through a transition; you are going through a metamorphosis. Transition is the process of going from one season to another; metamorphosis is not about changing seasons but changing you.* I personalized the message and shared it with the team as we all sat there sort of shell-shocked. I continued, "The caterpillar is attached to the earth, but we have endured the dark season of the cocoon to be transformed into a butterfly and be attached to the heavens. The caterpillar spends about two weeks in the cocoon before emerging with wings and a passion to fly. *We are emerging from this 'COVID cocoon' with a passion to attach ourselves to our heavenly calling.*" If you are going through a dark season, I want to encourage you to stick your head out of your cocoon because you are about to fly!

METAMORPHOSIS

I left the meeting realizing that I had spoken out of prophetic revelation; but, frankly, I wasn't sure how all the pain of our past "cocoon" was yielding a glorious new future for Bethel or for myself, for that matter. Yet I had never been so thoroughly convinced of the accuracy of a prophetic declaration in my life. I spent the next few months meditating on the word *metamorphosis* and praying for practical insights into leading our teams forward to embrace the reality of this transformation. The apostle Paul pioneered this spiritual concept of our divine metamorphosis when he declared, "*Do not be conformed to this world, but be transformed by the renewing of your mind*" (Romans 12:2). The Greek word for *"transformed"* in this verse is *metamorphoō*,[2] from which we get our English words *transfigured* and *transformed*.

This verse teaches us that metamorphosis begins in our minds. Or, more accurately, in our thought life. We must leave caterpillar mindsets—earthly, finite, limited thinking—and begin to embrace a heavenly mindset based on the superior reality of our transcended position in Christ. Metaphorically speaking, we are the butterfly, who does not leave the cocoon of darkness bruised or battered by his past ugly life, relegated to the dirt of his earthly existence. *No!* Instead, bearing no resemblance to his former life of dust and filth, he rises in the glory of his majestic wings and catches the currents of his heavenly call. He lives with no regrets of his former condition, realizing intuitively that it was the caterpillar that became the cocoon and provided the womb of metamorphosis necessary for divine transfiguration that ultimately yielded the wings of the dawn of a new era.

WE MUST LEAVE CATERPILLAR
MINDSETS—EARTHLY, FINITE, LIMITED
THINKING—AND BEGIN TO EMBRACE
A HEAVENLY MINDSET BASED ON
THE SUPERIOR REALITY OF OUR
TRANSCENDED POSITION IN CHRIST.

In fact, Paul went on to explain to the Colossians the practical aspects of metamorphosis:

---

2. "G3339–metamorphoō–Strong's Greek Lexicon (NASB95)," Blue Letter Bible, accessed June 10, 2025, https://www.blueletterbible.org/lexicon/g3339/nasb95/mgnt/0-1/.

Therefore if you have been raised up with Christ, keep seeking the things above, where Christ is, seated at the right hand of God. Set your mind on the things above, not on the things that are on earth. For you have died and your life is hidden with Christ in God. When Christ, who is our life, is revealed, then you also will be revealed with Him in glory. (Colossians 3:1–4)

My mind explodes with possibility as I meditate on this concept of processing our worldly challenges from the position of our heavenly seat, thinking future-present and not reacting to the troubles of earth but responding in the authority of transcended reality. What would it be like to live from heaven to earth, leaving the limitations of the perspective of the caterpillar, who views life crawling on his belly? How would it feel to fly above the problems of life, to be able to detach from earth long enough to view the world through the Father's eyes? Can you imagine letting go of the pain of the past and embracing His promise of prosperity?

At this point, you might be thinking that I'm so heavenly minded that I'm no earthly good. Or maybe that this is hyper-spiritual thinking that isn't relevant to everyday life. I get it! I also understand that life is challenging and that many people escape into fantasy or live in denial, out of touch with reality, and exist irresponsibly. I'm not suggesting that we detach from reality but that we view our earthly existence from a more accurate perspective. This will likely cause us to question the reality of our powerless perspective and thus lead us to become "solutionaries" who tap into "Spiritategies" (my term for "Spirit-led strategies") and the power of the age to come. The Bible is filled with stories of everyday people who experienced heavenly solutions for impossible situations because they lived with a great awareness of the Spirit realm. We will talk more about supernatural interventions later in this book; but, for now, I want to challenge you to begin the metamorphosis by allowing God to transform your darkness into a cocoon that will give way to His Spirit's work in your life.

A RACE TO RUN, AND A FIGHT TO WIN!

Maybe you are saying to yourself, "I'm not called to be a leader, and so I don't relate to the life of someone who is leading a church and/or a movement." But the truth is, everyone is meant to take leadership of their own life and circumstances. Moreover, your Father is the King of the world; therefore, you have been called and commissioned to take part in discipling the nations. Remember David? He was minding his father's sheep when the prophet Samuel showed up at his house and anointed him as king. (See 1 Samuel 16:1–13.) How about the famous Bible character Gideon, who was a frustrated farmer when the angel of the Lord called him a *"valiant warrior"* and commissioned him to lead the armies of Israel? (See Judges 6:11–16.) Let's not forget the twelve disciples, who were fishermen, farmers, tax collectors, and activists the day before Jesus showed up and said, "Follow Me." As for me, in my early years, I was a small-time businessman eking out a living in a town called Weaverville. (Think of it: *Weaver*-ville…I mean, a place named after weavers is not exactly a status symbol. In fact, we used to say that Weaverville was the place where elephants go to die!) Furthermore, I had no formal education beyond high school (from which I barely graduated), and I have had two serious nervous breakdowns. Not exactly leadership material, I'd say!

You may not be called to lead thousands or to preach from a podium. You might never be well-known or famous. But you are the King's kid, and that means you have a race to run and a fight to win! You are destined to win, called to succeed, and anointed to destroy the works of the devil. With Jesus living in you, you are a force to be reckoned with, an armored-up warrior, and more than a conqueror. Like Gideon, you may feel like a failed, insignificant human; but Jesus calls you His friend. Therefore, your life matters to God and to everyone with whom you come into contact.

3

BEYOND THE
STRATOSPHERE

I told you about the first meetings we had at Bethel during the hellish COVID season. Those meetings became known as the "As One" meetings, where I received the prophetic word about the coming metamorphosis. We all began to seek the Lord for more direction. In the midst of our search, I had a vision of a rocket ship going to the moon. I felt compelled to watch footage of NASA's first manned moon launch, which was Apollo 11. I found several YouTube videos and watched them over and over again. Although I was enamored by the moon shot, I wasn't sure why I was watching these videos until a profound theme began to emerge, which I will reveal in a moment.

LIFT OFF!

I was excited to share my discovery with the team, so I brought a YouTube video of the Apollo 11 launch to the next "As One" meeting and cued it up on our big-screen TV. Without any explanation, just as our seventy people got seated, I turned off the lights, cranked up the sound, and pushed PLAY.

If you've never experienced the awe of the Apollo 11 launch, I highly encourage you to explore the incredible footage available on YouTube. But, for now, let me bring the moment to life for you.

Imagine the NASA control room filled with engineers and scientists dressed in white lab coats. Their gazes are fixed on the TV monitors, viewing the rocket ship on the launchpad, which is preparing for liftoff. One by one, various members of the launch team check their given area of responsibility and verbalize their approval, affirming that everything is a "go." As each one presents their verbal authorization, the excitement in the room grows exponentially more intense. Finally, after all the members have signaled their approval, the countdown begins, narrated by NASA's chief of public affairs: "Ten, nine...Ignition sequence starts..." The sound of the boosters fills the air. The narrator continues, "Six, five, four, three, two, one, zero! All engines go." The rocket bursts to life, shaking the ground as it lifts off. The narrator exclaims, "LIFT OFF! We have lift off!"

The rocket climbs higher and higher, piercing through the clouds and pushing past the Earth's atmosphere with unstoppable force. Flames trail beneath as it ascends toward the edge of space. About two minutes after the launch, something profound happens; something I never understood before unfolded right before my eyes. The lower stage boosters, now spent, detach from the rocket and fall away, tumbling back toward Earth as mission control confirms their successful separation. What I discovered that morning is that, when the rocket leaves the stratosphere, all the fuel in the boosters has been expelled; thus, the boosters have served their purpose and need to be ejected. What was necessary to propel the rocket to that point is actually a dead-weight deterrent beyond the stratosphere. The boosters must be released for the rocket to reach its ultimate destination.

FLAMED OUT

My mind began to explode with revelation; metaphorically speaking, I understood for the first time that we aren't going to reach our divine destination if we don't let go of encumbrances that were necessary in the previous epoch season. Those "boosters" have expelled their fuel and have flamed out in the greater purpose of our divine providence. In fact, not only are the boosters no longer propelling us forward, but they don't even have the energy to carry their own weight! They must be released to the ocean of irrelevance as a relic of significance from a former season of life.

WE AREN'T GOING TO REACH OUR DIVINE DESTINATION IF WE DON'T LET GO OF ENCUMBRANCES THAT WERE NECESSARY IN THE PREVIOUS EPOCH SEASON.

The writer of the book of Hebrews captured this concept when he exhorted us to become race-ready. He wrote, *"Therefore, since we have so great a cloud of witnesses surrounding us, let us also lay aside every encumbrance and the sin which so easily entangles us, and let us run with endurance the race that is set before us"* (Hebrews 12:1). The Greek word translated as *"encumbrance"* is *ogkos*, which can mean "bulk," "mass," or "weight."[3] I've always understood that sin derails us from running a good race by entangling us in guilt and undermining our noble identity. But encumbrances? I mean, are there things that entangle us that aren't sin but are *equally* inhibiting our purpose? "What might those be?" I wondered.

---

3. "G3591–ogkos–Strong's Greek Lexicon (NASB95)," Blue Letter Bible, accessed June 10, 2025. https://www.blueletterbible.org/lexicon/g3591/nasb95/mgnt/0-1/.

Jesus shared a parable that is insightful for unearthing the encumbrance dynamic that limits our productivity and undermines our purpose. He told the story of a vineyard, explaining it like this: *"I am the true vine, and My Father is the vinedresser. Every branch in Me that does not bear fruit, He takes away; and every branch that bears fruit, He prunes it so that it may bear more fruit"* (John 15:1–2). He went on to clarify that we (believers) are the branches that are being pruned back or cut off.

My Uncle Sally owned a small vineyard when I was a teenager, and I used to work on his farm during the summer. I learned a little bit about vines and vinedressers in those days. A vine, left unattended, will spend all its energy extending its branches until it literally has no energy left to produce leaves, much less fruit. If you discover an unattended branch twenty feet long, for example, the first five feet of the branch will likely have grapes on it, the next three feet will have only leaves, and the last twelve feet will be just a long stick. In other words, a grapevine becomes a stick tree if it gets overextended! If you don't prune the branch all the way back to its fruitfulness, the vine's capacity to produce fruit will be siphoned off by the energy it takes to grow sticks.

I want to assure you that no farmer prunes in order to produce less fruit! Farmers prune with a promise in mind—the promise of an exponential harvest. Metaphorically speaking, pruning back the encumbrances of our lives or cutting off branches that were once fruitful but have become unproductive, life-sucking, nourishment-stealing sticks of irrelevance can be painful. Yet, left unchecked, they will siphon off the life flow of our entire vine, leaving us useless, weak, and feeble.

I am concerned that we have canonized the "boosters" of our former fruitful seasons and continue to hold fast to certain methods and modes as if they are sacred or holy. Yet the truth is that many of these methods and modes are actually empty containers of powerless obligation, which we drag along behind us like a ball and chain in a lifeless journey of exasperation and frustration. This was my message that day in the "As One" meeting when I stopped the Apollo 11 video and shouted abruptly, "What are the 'boosters' of our lives that were so important to our success but have lost their purpose in the light of this new epoch metamorphosis?" A passionate dialogue ensued among the team members as each person offered their insights into which areas, once so full of life and love, had now become fruitless efforts of religion.

THE JOURNEY OUT OF YESTERDAY

The truth is, it takes great courage to leave the illusion of our success when our boosters have obviously run out of fuel. People waste a lot of effort and resources trying to sustain something that only weighs them down. There is no shame in letting go of something that was once fruitful but is now just a fruitless vine. We often blame others and thus rotate through an endless carousel of fruitless fixes and never solve the problem. This cycle can go on for years as we brand—and then abandon—each new fix.

Of course, not all our failures are caused by boosters that have simply run out of gas. Many of us fail because of poor character, bad attitudes, and/or a lack of effort. Some people become disillusioned and stop seeking God, or they fail to move in spiritual power or to sincerely love others.

PEOPLE WHO RUN OUT OF CAPACITY

Yet one of the most painful situations a person can find themselves in happens when, in the transition from the "atmosphere" to "space," the empty boosters are other people. What I mean is this: sometimes the people who were catalytic in a former season become irrelevant to the new era of opportunity. Often, it's not that they're lazy or irresponsible; it's simply that they are incapable of fulfilling the necessary roles that present themselves in our emerging environment. Their gift mix no longer matches and thus is not helpful in the new challenges we face; or they have a talent gap, a lack of experience, or a limited capacity of soul.

Let me give you an example I faced in my world as my responsibility grew in my job. In 1998, my wife, Kathy, and I helped to start the Bethel School of Supernatural Ministry. As you might imagine, with a name like that, we weren't trying to attract the multitudes; we were looking for the rare radical who wanted to lay down their life for Jesus, no matter the cost. Our first pioneer class began with thirty-seven students and a small but amazing team of volunteer leaders. These leaders truly loved the students and spent hours of one-on-one time with them. But something nobody anticipated took place: our little school *blew up*! By year five, we had over six hundred students. Furthermore, the school was doubling about every two years. In year six, we received a certification from Homeland Security that authorized us to accept international students. Within a few years, we became the largest international vocational school in American history! As mentioned in chapter 2, more than two thousand students attended every year from over seventy nations.

One of the side effects of this explosive growth was that the personal capacity of many of our original leaders was no match for the level of responsibility and authority necessary to lead the school. It wasn't long after this exponential growth that many of our original leaders left. Some of them faced months of stress-related sicknesses before they finally quit. Migraine headaches, insomnia, high levels of anxiety, and panic attacks became common among our leaders. The truth is, all of us were being stretched, and this exposed cracks in our foundations. Some of us were able to grow from the pressure and increase our capacity over time; others simply ran out of fuel and flamed out as they painfully crash-landed. This didn't mean that God's purposes for them had ended. He had a new season for them, too; their own metamorphosis required finding the different path He had prepared for them in the fullness of their own unique gifts and capacities.

TAKING THE PAINFUL PATH FORWARD

These are just some of the types of challenges we may face as we navigate the moon shot of our divine destination. Growing pains can be so complex and severely intense that they paralyze us, and we do nothing at all. Thus, we give in to the often repeated but seldom true idiom, "Things will work themselves out." It's true that things work themselves out, but the outcome of inaction is usually not positive. Marriage problems hardly ever magically get better by themselves; they more often end in divorce. A personal or corporate financial crisis left unattended will usually wind up in bankruptcy, not in prosperity. When we refuse to lead ourselves well, we are like a garden left to cultivate itself—soon weeds and rodents destroy what was once a promising environment. Adam was placed in the garden of Eden to *"cultivate it and keep it"* (Genesis 2:15). Think about it: long before Adam sinned, Eden's garden still needed a caretaker. What are the chances that our situations are going to get better if we don't put on our big boy (or big girl) pants and do something about them?

FIVE QUESTIONS TO HELP YOU GET STARTED

Our response to the need for metamorphosis—whether that metamorphosis is a result of gradual shifts or sudden changes that come in unrelenting waves—will have the greatest impact on how we learn to *just stand* in the midst of both crises and the natural rhythms of life. How do we begin the process of responding well to metamorphosis? Here are five questions you can answer that will help you get the process started:

1. *What is your moon shot?* Often, in a season of metamorphosis, our prior moon shot (that is, our overarching goal or purpose) needs to be changed or at least modified. As we have seen, we can waste a lot of time and energy trying to accomplish something that was necessary in the caterpillar season but is currently either impossible or irrelevant in the new butterfly pilgrimage of our divine purpose. Consequently, it's paramount that we reexamine our overarching purpose *before* we waste our energy on finding a new process.

2. *What are the "boosters" of your life that were important to your previous success but have lost their purpose in the light of this new epoch metamorphosis?* As I pointed out earlier, this type of change can involve a very painful process in which a loyalty to methods, memories, or manpower can blind us to the truth of how to move forward—a truth that's often hiding in plain sight. But the pain of letting go of the past must be measured against the costs of missing our purpose in God. Furthermore, not only will our inaction affect our present condition, but the future purpose of the coming generations will also be undermined and/or derailed. We simply must not allow this to happen.

OUR RESPONSE TO THE NEED FOR METAMORPHOSIS WILL HAVE THE GREATEST IMPACT ON HOW WE LEARN TO *JUST STAND* IN THE MIDST OF BOTH CRISES AND THE NATURAL RHYTHMS OF LIFE.

---

3. *Which wise people can help you navigate this new metamorphosis?* Solomon said, *"In abundance of counselors there is victory"* (Proverbs 24:6)—but those *"counselors"* must be chosen prayerfully and carefully; otherwise, the outcome will be skewed. It's important to hear from a variety of perspectives so that every possible dynamic is represented well and listened to. *But* there are certain people whose opinion is so predictively negative that they can completely paralyze the process. Therefore, be sure to use discernment.

4. *How should the structure you live in change to facilitate the destiny of your new season?* The structure you live and work in is paramount to your success as a believer. The structure should first be specifically designed by evaluating your strengths and weaknesses and the season you are living in, and then developed and deployed to cover your weaknesses and empower your strengths. Let me share a great word picture with you that I've used for years to help illustrate how wise structures affect our productivity and thus determine our level of success. A smart contractor in our city of Redding built a new building for Shasta College, a local community college. When he finished the facility, he planted lawn all the way around the building. A year later, he built sidewalks where the faculty and students had worn out the lawn in their treks to and from classes, dorms, and other areas of community life. In this way, the sidewalks facilitated the destiny of the faculty and students. This is a beautiful illustration of the important impact that structures have on the efficiency and effectiveness of our life. You can have the fastest car in the world, but if there are no paved roads to your ultimate destination, your journey will probably be slow at best and treacherous at worst. If you are stuck in an antiquated structure designed for "caterpillars" and not for "butterflies," there's likely not going to be much "high flying" going on in your life!

5. *What needs to change in you to reach your destiny and fulfill your purpose?* Maybe the toughest part of going into an epoch metamorphosis is not what is happening around you but what needs to happen within you. In fact, the kingdom within you actually manifests around you...not the other way around. Therefore, the most important and dynamic catalyst of change is *you!* Change—especially radical change—can be incredibly difficult. To make things even more challenging, you can't become what you haven't already seen and heard, and there are often few, if any, people modeling the kind of inner transformation

necessary to bust out of the stale mold of past-present thinking. Furthermore, if the thing that needs to be overhauled or let go of in your life is the place where you have prospered in a former epoch season, it's tough to convince yourself to shed it.

DIFFERENCE MAKER

My friend Banning Liebscher, the founding pastor of Jesus Culture, says, "The difference between people who do something and people who don't is that people who do something, do something!" Procrastination is the assassination of revelation. I know that sounds like a line from a rap song, but it's true. We can think about change, analyze it, and research it, but nothing is going to change until we do *something* about it. We must move forward, whether we take baby steps or elephant steps. But whatever we do, we have to find the grit to step past our fear of the unknown and make progress every day.

Well, since we're talking about elephants…do you know how to eat an elephant? One bite at a time! Let's not allow the elephant to live in our room—let's eat the dang thing.

4

THE POWER OF AN ECOSYSTEM

*S**poiler alert: what we cultivate dominates!* Let me begin with a simple illustration. One day, I sat in the claw-foot tub in the bathroom of my bedroom, enjoying the hot water that enveloped my tired body. But the longer I soaked, the cooler the water became, until I finally had to either get out or add more hot water to the tub. As I contemplated the coolness of my situation, I realized that, regardless of what temperature it started out being, the water in the bath would eventually become room temperature—not a degree hotter or colder. "Why?" you may ask. Because the bathroom itself had an ecosystem that maintained an overall climate, while the bathtub had no such ecosystem (it wasn't a hot tub). I had set the thermostat to 70 degrees before I got in the tub; therefore, 70 degrees would become the prevailing temperature of everything in the room. It's not that 70 degrees is, in itself, a dominant temperature.

What made it the prevailing temperature was the ecosystem in the room, which, in this case, was the heating and air-conditioning (HVAC) system.

CREATING ECOSYSTEMS

My bathroom's ecosystem is adjusted by a thermostat and maintained by a complex HVAC system. The system was specifically designed to take into account several factors, like the size of the room, the percentage of window-to-wall space, the height of the ceiling, the climate of the area, and so on. Furthermore, the ecosystem in my bathroom works inside a larger ecosystem called Mother Nature! My HVAC system isn't powerful enough to keep my entire property—both the house and the yard—at a certain temperature; it needs the walls, windows, and ceiling of the house to insulate the bathroom from the exterior climate. Therefore, those components are also part of the ecosystem. If I open the sliding door on a 100-degree day, my air conditioner doesn't have the capacity to maintain a comfortable temperature inside.

IF YOU CHANGE THE ECOSYSTEM, YOU WILL CHANGE THE OUTCOME.

Now, let's think about our life as an ecosystem and our heart as the bedroom of our soul. The first question we must ask ourselves is this: Am I a thermometer (reflecting) or a thermostat (regulating)? In other words, metaphorically speaking, do I even have a heating and air-conditioning system in my soul, or do I just absorb the temperature of the room (my current mindset and circumstances)? Jesus said, "*I know your deeds, that you are neither cold nor hot; I wish that you were cold or hot. So because you are lukewarm, and neither hot nor cold, I will spit you out of My mouth*" (Revelation 3:15–16). It takes effort and energy to be either hot or cold. Something that is lukewarm is said to be "room temperature"—and being lukewarm is the proverbial "thermometer life" born from a heart that reflects the culture but makes no effort to transform it.

Everything in life that *perpetuates*—be it good or bad—has an ecosystem. If you change the ecosystem, you will change the outcome. For example, if I lied once to someone, that's an incident, yet if I lie all the time, that's an ecosystem. In both cases, lying is wrong, but repentance from a false ecosystem, resulting in real change in my life, has a very specific journey. If I lie habitually but have a desire to become a righteous, noble person of character, it's unlikely that I will be able to discipline myself out of lying, as this habit is probably a manifestation of an unhealthy ecosystem within me. Consequently, permanent change will take place only when I discover the dysfunctional ecosystem within me and make adjustments to create a new, healthy ecosystem.

For instance, let's say I allow the Spirit to search my heart, and I unearth the fact that I was raised in a culture of severe punishment, and I realize that I'm afraid of the consequences of telling the truth when I've failed. I've become a habitual liar—not because I'm dishonest but because I'm afraid. Fear has created an ecosystem inside me in which the outcome is lying! In my heating and air-conditioning metaphor, lying is like cold air blowing out of the vents, but the fear of punishment is the HVAC system. Furthermore, if I live with people who actually do punish me when I fail, this might be compared to walls and a ceiling that imprison my soul and complete the ecosystem of deception that says, "People who fail deserve to be punished." Ecosystems of the soul are *always* rooted in belief systems. If you truly want to change the way you live, you *must* change what you believe!

THINGS THAT PREDETERMINE OUR CAUSE OF DEATH

With all this in mind, let's take a look at the "sword life" articulated by Jesus. He said, in effect, "If you live by the sword, you will die by the sword." (See Matthew 26:52.) The way we live, love, and war becomes an ecosystem that predetermines whether we will flourish or flounder, be bonded or broken, or be a victor over or a victim of the world around us. The truth is, it's not so much what happens *to* us that determines our future success or failure but what happens *in* us. Revenge, unforgiveness, jealousy, and selfishness are just a few of the unrighteous and unauthorized swords that can destroy our souls and undermine our legacy.

Here is the context of Jesus's statement: the temple soldiers, led by Judas, had come to arrest Him. Peter pulled out his sword (which Jesus had told him to bring; see Luke 22:35–38) and struck the slave of the high priest and cut off his ear. (See Matthew 26:51.) Jesus intervened immediately and said to him, *"Put your sword back into its place; for all those who take up the sword shall perish by the sword"* (verse 52). He went on to say, *"Or do you think that I cannot appeal to My Father, and He will at once put at My disposal more than twelve legions of angels?"* (verse 53). You can predict your cause of death by determining whether you will *respond to* or *react to* life's circumstances!

Okay, let's process this together. I said that all ecosystems of the soul begin with what we believe about our situation. Jesus believed that His heavenly Father protected Him, and therefore He responded in peace and refused to protect Himself. His response to Peter about angels being at His disposal unearthed the core values that were the foundation of His ecosystem and thus determined His behavior. Now let's think about Peter for a minute. A few hours earlier, Jesus had told him to get a sword. Peter had already verbalized his unwavering commitment and courage to Jesus. So, it's safe to say that Jesus's sword instructions played into Peter's belief that they were supposed to defend themselves—or, more accurately, that Peter was supposed to defend them since Jesus had no sword. Yet Jesus addressed something exponentially deeper than the violent episode that unfolded before Him that fateful night in the garden. He destroyed the ecosystem that was trying to surface among His disciples—the conviction that they must defend their faith with violence. He injected truth into His young, zealous band of brothers: *"Do you think that I cannot appeal to My Father, and He will at once put at My disposal more than twelve legions of angels?"*

It's revealing that He posed the question in the negative tense: *"Do you think that I **cannot** appeal to My Father...?"* In other words, your thinking is wrong...your framework of beliefs is flawed...your reaction is the result of a defective ecosystem. Jesus didn't just correct Peter's behavior; He corrected his belief system! This one incident likely laid the foundation for the disciples to become reformers rather than violent activists!

Furthermore, Jesus refused to let the action of the crowd provoke a reaction from Him. He was acting out His *"Do not resist an evil person; but whoever slaps you on your right cheek, turn the other to him also"* sermon. (See Matthew 5:39.) Jesus wasn't teaching His disciples to be passive. He was teaching them to live from virtues and values, and not to react to the actions of others! When we allow the actions of others to prompt our reactions, we have given control of ourselves over to the people around us. This again is the lukewarm life of having no inner ecosystem dictating the temperature of our soul but having a thermometer existence of reflecting the attitudes and actions demonstrated in our environment.

ECOSYSTEMS EXPLAINED

Let me describe the simple ecosystem cycle of *disconnection* as an example of how the hamster wheel of dysfunction feeds itself. So, first I feel unworthy; therefore, I feel ashamed, so I hide; when I hide, I feel disconnected; when I am disconnected, I feel unworthy; consequently, I feel ashamed...and on and on the cycle goes. To break the power of the ecosystem of disconnection, I must deal with the lie that I am *unworthy.* Jesus said, *"You will know the truth, and the truth will make you free"* (John 8:32). The Greek root word translated as *"truth"* in this passage is *alētheia*, which can be defined as "in reality"![4] So, the verse might be read in this way: "You will know *reality*, and *reality* will make you free!" Many people try to change their behavior in order to exit the hamster wheel, which, in the case of my illustration, would mean for me to stop hiding. But hiding isn't the root of my disconnection; believing I am unworthy is the foundation of my prison of solitary confinement. The apostle Paul put it best: *"Do not be conformed to this world, but be transformed by the renewing of your mind"* (Romans 12:2). You can't change your life, but if you change your mind, God will transform your life! In this situation, I must apply God's truth to the lie of my unworthiness to transform the ecosystem of disconnection. Here is a simple way to think about ecosystems: Cause + Reaction = Ecosystem. Cause + Analyze + Respond = Altered Ecosystem!

JOHN 8:32 MIGHT BE READ IN THIS WAY:
"YOU WILL KNOW *REALITY*, AND *REALITY*
WILL MAKE YOU FREE!"

CORE VALUES VERSUS HIGH VALUES

Core values are the most prominent factor in developing the ecosystem of our heart. Core values are the lenses through which we view life. In the example of disconnection I just shared, my core value is that I am unworthy. Metaphorically speaking, I am viewing the world through glasses that have scratched lenses. It's important to understand that my core values are not *what* I see but the *way* I see it and, therefore, the way in which I interpret reality.

---

4. "G225—alētheia—Strong's Greek Lexicon (KJV)," Blue Letter Bible, accessed July 3, 2025, https://www.blueletterbible.org/lexicon/g225/kjv/tr/0-1/.

Furthermore, my *high* values are not necessarily my *core* values! That distinction might sound confusing, but let me give you a simple example to explain it. Let's say that my high value is that God *always* takes care of me. I memorize Philippians 4:19, which says, *"God will supply all your needs according to His riches in glory in Christ Jesus,"* and I make it my motto for life. Heck, I even have it tattooed on my chest over my heart. But two months after I get the tattoo, I don't have the money to pay my rent, and I begin to worry myself into a panic. Okay, we have all been in similar situations, but let me point out a life-changing truth as it pertains to this example. In this case, "God always provides for me" is my high value; it's what I want to believe, or maybe even what I am determined to believe. *But* worry has unearthed that my core value is actually that God doesn't always provide for me!

Let me be clear: I am not trying to shame anyone here; I'm trying to give us the tools we need to make a prison break, leave a life of bondage, and *stand strong* in freedom. Core values are the lens of my heart; high values are the intellectual agreements I make in my head with either truths or lies. If my high values are actually rooted in truth like the Philippians passage I quoted, then the goal is to assimilate these high values into my being until they become the core values of my heart and thus the lens of my life.

SON GLASSES

Jesus said, *"So take care how you listen"* (Luke 8:18). He often warned us about what we listen to (which we will get to in a minute); yet, in this passage, the emphasis is not on *what* we listen to but *how* we listen. I often say that all of us speak with an accent, but we usually don't know we have an accent until we meet someone who speaks with a different accent. Then we tend to think *they* are the one with the accent. But I'd like to propose that we also hear and see with an accent—a cultural and experiential bent that affects the way we process life. Furthermore, we often question what we see or hear, but we seldom question *how* we process this information. For example, if we are prejudiced against a particular ethnic group, it will affect the way we process information about them, influencing what we think is fact or fallacy. Therefore, core values are the accent of our hearts!

Now let's take this a bit deeper. Jesus also said, *"Take care what you listen to"* (Mark 4:24). Our brain has a filter known as the *thalamus*. This part of the brain determines what we listen to or reject, what we believe to be true or false, what we value, and the experiences we welcome or discard. This is our reality filter. We pay attention to only a small portion of the information presented to us every day and reject most of it as unnecessary, untrue, unhealthy, or hurtful. This process is known as *selective filtering*, and we do it thousands of times a day. For example, if I have an interest in cars, watching the traffic crawl along in a busy upscale city might be like watching a car show for me. For everybody else, it's just congestion as they deal with the frustration of a delayed ride home. This simple illustration demonstrates how our interests and biases shape the way we perceive the world. Our interests help to dictate our internal filters, emphasizing what matters to us in life while ignoring what doesn't.

Our heart is the master of our thalamus, creating the core values for our selective filtering, determining what is—to us—real, valuable, worthless, fake, fantasy, and so on. Consequently, we tend to see what we are prepared to see, what we are looking for, and what we value. We tend to miss the things we don't believe in or don't value. This causes us to see things not as they are but as we are!

Years ago, I had an eye-opening experience that really drove this concept home for me. I was at a conference attended by about a thousand people where the speaker was teaching us about the effect core values have on the way we view life. He brought a barrel containing roughly thirty colored flags up front, and he asked us to count the number of gold flags as he slowly rotated the container. Next, he instructed us to close our eyes and tell him how many red flags there were in the barrel. Well, all of us had been looking for gold flags, so we had hardly noticed the red flags that were as easily viewed in the barrel. The lesson was crystal clear. Again, we see what we are prepared to see. But it's our core values that determine what we are prepared to see!

THE INFLUENCE AND FRUIT OF OUR CORE VALUES

With that said, let me give you a few key statements about the influence core values have on *how* we think and *what* we think:

+ Core values are the foundational principles of our lives by which we interpret reality and truth.

+ Core values are the lenses that determine the way in which we see life. They are the interpreters of the events of our world. When something happens to us or around us, our core values dictate how we explain these events to ourselves and others.

+ Our core values set the boundaries for our behavior. They tell us how to act in our ministry, family relationships, friendships, business dealings, and conflicts. Our core values are the referees in our relationships.

+ Our core values are the prophets of our destiny. They dictate what we allow ourselves to desire. They decide what is important for us to accomplish in our lives.

+ Our core values determine the way we see God.

+ Our core values interpret how the events in our life relate to God. They determine which circumstances in life we attribute to God, the devil, man, or chance.

We can't change what we refuse to confront, and we can't confront what we can't see or perceive. Therefore, it's necessary for each of us to *question our reality* to determine if *our truth* is THE TRUTH! How do we know if we are living with healthy core values? Well, that's a great question. The answer is to do an honest fruit-check of our life, because fruit always reveals the root of the ecosystem of our soul.

Here are a few examples of bad fruit that points to core values that are rooted in lies:

+ *Hopelessness*: Any thought in our lives that doesn't inspire hope is rooted in a lie.

+ *Worry*: Worry is a squatter living rent free in our minds and destroying our house of faith. Worry plants in our brain weed-seeds of destructive possibilities, which infect our imagination with movies of mayhem and madness. I want to make worry an unwelcome vagabond who finds no habitation in our yard of possibility.

+ *Fear*: Fear often masquerades as wisdom, but it's actually a cowardly vagrant, unwilling to live in the shelter of responsibility and perseverance.

+ *Bitterness*: Unforgiveness, offense, hatred, anger, and related emotions are all root rotters and grave robbers. They continually dig up corpses of unresolved or wrongly resolved relational conflict, creating graveyards full of the unearthed skeletons of relationships gone bad.

I could go on and on, yet my goal here is for us to see the bad fruit in our lives and then do a root inspection to determine the cause of the spiritual sickness that's stealing the abundant life promised to us by our Lord. (See John 10:10.) In fact, as I write this paragraph, I have become aware that one of the most powerful lies that many of us believe is that suffering somehow makes us holy or at least acceptable to Jesus. As we will see in the next chapter, suffering is inevitable on this side of heaven, but the truth is that *"the kingdom of God is not eating and drinking, but righteousness and peace and joy in the Holy Spirit"* (Romans 14:17)!

POWERFUL CORE VALUES

Here are some examples of healthy core values from the Bible that will grow great fruit in our lives:

+ All things are working in our favor; therefore, when things are not going our way, we know God will still use the situation for our good.

> *We know that God causes all things to work together for good to those who love God, to those who are called according to His purpose.* (Romans 8:28)

+ God loved us before we loved Him, so He doesn't love us because we perform well; He loves us *all* the time.

> *We love, because He first loved us.* (1 John 4:19)

+ Fear is not a part of God's kingdom. Consequently, God doesn't bully us into obedience; He woos us by His love.

> *There is no fear in love; but perfect love casts out fear, because fear involves punishment, and the one who fears is not perfected in love.* (1 John 4:18)

+ God has plans to bless us; therefore, I live in hopeful expectation of His great plan for my life.

> *"For I know the plans that I have for you," declares the* Lord, *"plans for welfare and not for calamity to give you a future and a hope."* (Jeremiah 29:11)

+ We are special and holy people handpicked by His Majesty to be part of His royal family.

> *But you are a chosen race, a royal priesthood, a holy nation, a people for God's own possession, so that you may proclaim the excellencies of Him who has called you out of darkness into His marvelous light.* (1 Peter 2:9)

+ We are equipped to overcome and overpower anything evil that the enemy raises up against us. That's why we are conquerors, not cowards; and victors, not victims.

> *But in all these things we overwhelmingly conquer through*
> *Him who loved us.* (Romans 8:37)

+ We are called to destroy the works of the devil, so we are on the offense, not living our life afraid of Satan.

> *The one who practices sin is of the devil; for the devil has*
> *sinned from the beginning. The Son of God appeared for this*
> *purpose, to destroy the works of the devil.* (1 John 3:8)

+ We were born to rule; therefore, we are powerful, wise, noble people.

> *Then the sovereignty, the dominion and the greatness of all*
> *the kingdoms under the whole heaven will be given to the*
> *people of the saints of the Highest One; His kingdom will be*
> *an everlasting kingdom, and all the dominions will serve and*
> *obey Him.* (Daniel 7:27)

+ We have a friendship with God, so He enjoys being with us.

> *No longer do I call you slaves, for the slave does not know*
> *what his master is doing; but I have called you friends, for all*
> *things that I have heard from My Father I have made known*
> *to you.* (John 15:15)

+ Signs and wonders follow us. We leave a trail of healing and wholeness wherever we go.

> *These signs will accompany those who have believed: in My*
> *name they will cast out demons, they will speak with new*
> *tongues; they will pick up serpents, and if they drink any*
> *deadly poison, it will not hurt them; they will lay hands on*
> *the sick, and they will recover.* (Mark 16:17–18)

+ The Holy Spirit is tending the garden of our heart, which is becoming like Eden's orchard in the Spirit.

> *But the fruit of the Spirit is love, joy, peace, patience, kind-*
> *ness, goodness, faithfulness, gentleness, self-control; against*
> *such things there is no law.*   (Galatians 5:22–23)

Of course, this is in no way an exhaustive list of the biblical core values that we should embrace as the lens of our life. As I pointed out, it's just a sample of the kind of values that create healthy ecosystems in us and around us. As we assimilate these truths into our heart, we will begin to think differently; our attitude will change, and our actions will demonstrate a life of nobility.

PROACTIVELY DEVELOPING ECOSYSTEMS

It's not enough to reform our inner man; the kingdom within us must also positively affect the world around us. So, now that we have talked about developing a healthy ecosystem within us, let's examine how to further form the ecosystems of our surrounding environment. The apostle Paul said:

> *Do not be deceived, God is not mocked; for whatever a man sows,*
> *this he will also reap. For the one who sows to his own flesh will from*
> *the flesh reap corruption, but the one who sows to the Spirit will from*
> *the Spirit reap eternal life. Let us not lose heart in doing good, for in*
> *due time we will reap if we do not grow weary.* (Galatians 6:7–9)

Now let's get really practical. To Paul's point, if we sow corn, we are not going to reap apples; we are going to harvest corn. If we sow bitterness, anger, and selfishness into relationships, we are not going to harvest love, connection, and peace. Most likely, we are going to reap disconnection, mistrust, brokenness, and maybe even hatred. If we change the seed we plant, we will change the harvest we reap.

As we just read, Paul emphasized, *"Let us not lose heart in doing good, for in due time we will reap if we do not grow weary."* In other words, when we change our seed, it might take a while before we reap a different crop.

For example, if we were sowing to the flesh by planting weed-seeds in our garden of life (like unforgiveness, immorality, and violence), and we finally repent and begin sowing to the Spirit kindness, love, and gentleness, a change may not be immediate. It will likely take time before the environment we sowed into has a "crop" change. I like to say, "We are always eating last year's produce."

IT'S NOT ENOUGH TO REFORM OUR INNER MAN; THE KINGDOM WITHIN US MUST ALSO POSITIVELY AFFECT THE WORLD AROUND US.

POVERTY TO PROSPERITY

Ecosystems affect *every* area of life, including our finances; thus the adage, "If you need money, don't ask for money; ask why you need money." In other words, if we are short paying the rent this week, that's probably an incident. On the other hand, if we are always broke, that's likely the result of an ecosystem. The psalmist wrote, "*Those who sow in tears shall reap with joyful shouting. He who goes to and fro weeping, carrying his bag of seed, shall indeed come again with a shout of joy, bringing his sheaves with him*" (Psalm 126:5–6). The psalmist is telling the story of someone who needs the seed he is sowing to feed his children *now* because they are hungry; that's why he is sowing the seed with tears. But he understands that if he doesn't sow seed when he is broke, he will have no crop at all the next season. He would have destined himself and his family to long-term poverty because, without a crop, he would have no income.

Let me use the farm story to demonstrate how to *give* your way out of poverty and to help you understand more about ecosystems. Let's suppose you have a hundred acres of farmland, and you plant seed in fifty acres of it, using the rest of the seed you have for food. When harvesttime comes, you procure a good wheat crop from the fifty acres. The next year, you sacrifice some of the wheat seed you had planned to eat, and you plant seventy-five acres of the land. Of course, everything being equal, you now have a 50 percent larger crop than you had the year before. If you can live comfortably on the crops produced from only fifty acres, then you can use the extra twenty-five-acre harvest to reinvest in planting your entire one hundred acres. The more you plant, the more you harvest; and the more you harvest, the more seed you have to plant. Thus, soon you have broken the life cycle of poverty by sacrificing today's comfort for tomorrow's prosperity. (By the way, if you are interested in the subject of wealth, read my book, *Poverty, Riches and Wealth*.[5])

There are so many areas of life that have their own ecosystems that need to be cultivated, planted, and harvested. In fact, the subject could fill an entire book, but it will suffice to say that wherever we see long-term unhealthy areas in our life, we need to examine the ecosystems that are perpetuating the dysfunction and then make adjustments. As we discussed earlier, often, we will unearth a distorted belief system that is undermining our prosperity and derailing our divine destiny. Noble people who stand strong don't live and die by the sword; they are wise enough to make insightful inquiries and courageous enough to pursue real change in their lives. We are called to nobility, so let's live up to our full potential. Let us not just survive the storms of life but thrive in our walk with God—no matter what the circumstances may be.

---

5. Kris Vallotton, *Poverty, Riches and Wealth: Moving from a Life of Lack into True Kingdom Abundance* (Minneapolis, MN: Chosen, 2019).

5

THE SCIENCE OF SUFFERING

Sometimes, it's hard to move forward, even if we know the right thing to do, because of the severe level of suffering we're experiencing. Suffering is certainly a part of life; it's an unavoidable fact of living on planet Earth. Some Christians embrace suffering as if it's a badge of honor or a goal to be obtained, while others view it as a demonic plot—a sign of spiritual warfare that must be circumvented through prayer and fasting. Certainly, there are Scriptures to validate both of these polarized positions, and when they are viewed outside of their context, they can be confusing, at best, and disheartening when you are in the throes of pain. How do we "just stand" under these circumstances?

When the apostle Paul's credibility was questioned by some leaders who were trying to infiltrate the Corinthian church, Paul "went off" on them, using his own sufferings as the credentials that validated his apostleship in the lives of the Corinthians:

In whatever respect anyone else is bold—I speak in foolishness—I am just as bold myself. Are they Hebrews? So am I. Are they Israelites? So am I. Are they descendants of Abraham? So am I. Are they servants of Christ?—I speak as if insane—I more so; in far more labors, in far more imprisonments, beaten times without number, often in danger of death. Five times I received from the Jews thirty-nine lashes. Three times I was beaten with rods, once I was stoned, three times I was shipwrecked, a night and a day I have spent in the deep. I have been on frequent journeys, in dangers from rivers, dangers from robbers, dangers from my countrymen, dangers from the Gentiles, dangers in the city, dangers in the wilderness, dangers on the sea, dangers among false brethren; I have been in labor and hardship, through many sleepless nights, in hunger and thirst, often without food, in cold and exposure. Apart from such external things, there is the daily pressure on me of concern for all the churches. Who is weak without my being weak? Who is led into sin without my intense concern?

(2 Corinthians 11:21–29)

Again, the great apostle seemed to wear his suffering as a sign of nobility and to establish the credibility of his apostleship. Then, as if this "foolish" rant wasn't enough, Paul wrote to the Philippians, *"For to you it has been granted for Christ's sake, not only to believe in Him, but also to suffer for His sake, experiencing the same conflict which you saw in me, and now hear to be in me"* (Philippians 1:29–30). This was written by the man who had a PhD in suffering! I guess this is where the "suffering is a badge of honor" folks get their perspective. Here, Paul used the word *"granted,"* which is translated from the Greek word *charizomai* and can mean "to do a favor to."[6] Personally, I want to shout, "Please don't do me any favors, Lord!" Yet there must be advantages to suffering. Insights into eternity are often hidden in comfort, covered in convenience, and buried in the business of the pursuit of prosperity.

---

6. "G5483–charizomai–Strong's Greek Lexicon (kjv)," Blue Letter Bible, accessed June 10, 2025. https://www.blueletterbible.org/lexicon/g5483/kjv/tr/0-1/.

The truth is, there will be no suffering in heaven. Paul wrote:

Behold, I tell you a mystery; we will not all sleep, but we will all be changed, in a moment, in the twinkling of an eye, at the last trumpet; for the trumpet will sound, and the dead will be raised imperishable, and we will be changed. For this perishable must put on the imperishable, and this mortal must put on immortality.

(1 Corinthians 15:51–53)

The apostle John unearthed this revelation as well: "*He will wipe away every tear from their eyes; and there will no longer be any death; there will no longer be any mourning, or crying, or pain; the first things have passed away*" (Revelation 21:4). Hence, since there will be no suffering in heaven, there are some things that we can learn about the kingdom of God only on this side of eternity.

SINCE THERE WILL BE NO SUFFERING IN HEAVEN, THERE ARE SOME THINGS THAT WE CAN LEARN ABOUT THE KINGDOM OF GOD ONLY ON THIS SIDE OF ETERNITY.

SUFFERING HAS A WAY OF FINDING YOU

Personally, I don't think you have to pursue a life of suffering—it has a way of finding you sooner or later. Paul's collage of relentless agony wasn't a manifestation of a martyr's complex; I mean, he wasn't inviting a beating or hoping people would punish him. Instead, he was passionately preaching the gospel, refusing to be derailed by demented and/or demonized people, hypocritical religious leaders, or others who opposed him because they were jealous of his ministry. He was on a divine mission to spread the gospel, no matter what the cost to his personal safety or well-being. The price he paid reflected the value of the message he preached, and it demonstrated the depth of his conviction. For who would endure this level of agony for a lie or a fantasy?

Suffering was a common theme in the first-century church. Here is another case in point: Peter and some of the other apostles were preaching in the streets of Jerusalem, which ultimately led to their arrest. The Council (Sanhedrin) decided to let them off with a warning to stop their preaching. They flogged the apostles so it would be understood that they were serious about this warning. Here's the aftermath: *"So they went on their way from the presence of the Council, rejoicing that they had been considered worthy to suffer shame for His name."* Of course, the flogging didn't deter them; in fact, it actually inspired them—they *"kept right on teaching and preaching"* the gospel with passion! (See Acts 5:40–42.)

SUFFERING BECAUSE WE CARE

I know this may sound crazy, but the suffering of the early church reminds me of a story I read about Elon Musk. Although Musk is not a believer, his story can help us understand some of the valuable insights we can gain through the process of suffering. Musk is the owner of various companies, including Tesla, SpaceX, X, and many others. As of this writing, he is the richest man in the world![7] One of the most defining chapters in Musk's career came during the launch of the Tesla Model 3. Tesla was struggling to ramp up production, and the company came dangerously close to running out of money. Musk said that Tesla was "single-digit weeks" away from "death."[8] The situation became so dire that Musk, desperate to save his company, slept on the floor of the factory! In 2018, he was asked in an interview with Bloomberg why he slept

---

7. Chase Peterson-Withorn, Grace Chung, and Matt Durot, eds., "World's Billionaire's List: The Richest in 2025," *Forbes*, http://www.forbes.com/billionaires/.
8. Mike Allen and Jim VandeHei, "Elon Musk Says Tesla Came 'Within Single-Digit Weeks' of Death," *Axios*, November 26, 2018, https://www.axios.com/2018/11/26/elon-musk-tesla-death-bleeding-cash.

on the factory floor. He responded, "The reason I [slept] on the floor was not because I couldn't go across the road and be at the hotel. It was because I wanted my circumstance to be worse than anyone else at the company on purpose." Musk added, "Whatever pain they felt, I wanted mine to be worse. That's why I did it. And it makes a huge difference to people."[9] He explained, "I don't believe…people should be experiencing hardship while the CEO is like off on vacation."[10]

Musk's goal wasn't to suffer—his objective was to save his company. But the suffering was necessary to express to his employees how much he cared about the company, and to demonstrate the intense level of grit he was willing to endure to help it succeed. The suffering was a means to an end, not an end in itself.

Furthermore, sleeping on the factory floor gave Musk an intimate perspective of the production process, which led to many insights into the root causes of the challenges that were derailing Tesla's success. One of the positive side effects of the boss being in the trenches with the troops is that they bonded in the battle to save the company! Musk became one of them; the wall of wealth that separated the rich from the middle class crumbled in suffering and hard work as they fought together to save the company. Consequently, success wasn't found just in assembling cars; it was found in building a culture of caring for the company, the cars, and, most important, the people.[11] Moreover, the outcome of building great cars was that it helped to make Musk unimaginably rich!

THE GREATER PURPOSE OF SUFFERING

You might think it's disrespectful, unholy, or even outrageous to compare the early church's suffering to Musk's sleeping on the factory

---

9. Tom Randall, "'The Last Bet-the-Company Situation': Q&A with Elon Musk," Bloomberg: Business/Hyperdrive, July 13, 2018, https://www.bloomberg.com/news/features/2018-07-13/-the-last-bet-the-company-situation-q-amp-a-with-elon-musk.
10. "Tesla CEO Elon Musk Says Social Media, Artificial Intelligence Should Be Regulated," CBS News: CBS Mornings, April 11, 2018, https://www.cbsnews.com/news/elon-musk-tesla-model-3-problems-interview-today-2018-04-11/.
11. Randall, "'The Last Bet-the-Company Situation': Q&A with Elon Musk."

floor. I mean, Musk's suffering is a minor inconvenience when compared to the intense suffering of the first-century Christians who were fed to lions for entertainment, crucified on crosses, and burned alive on stakes along with their children. I certainly agree that there is a vast difference between these two examples; but, surprisingly, there is also a common thread in all sacrifice and suffering that serves a greater purpose. In Musk's case, the suffering led to insights into his company, his people, and the manufacturing process itself.

I had a similar experience during the COVID pandemic with our Bethel School of Ministry teams. In a previous chapter, I talked about how we were able to create a temporary online program so that our graduating students could receive their diplomas in the spring of 2020. But the governmental requirements at that time had shrunk our school from twenty-four hundred students to fourteen hundred students over a period of thirty days. Our international students, which make up 40 percent of our student body, weren't allowed in the United States, and many were required to go home. This was sad for all the obvious reasons, but one of the major side effects was the loss of $5.5 million in revenue, which meant massive layoffs for our team. Our team members are like family to me, and many of them had spouses and children whom they were supporting. Yet Bethel had no reserves, so the situation was dire. Furthermore, we were also hemorrhaging money from nearly every other department, which meant that we needed a miracle to keep our organization from a complete financial collapse. I took a drastic pay cut and spent the nights in prayer, trying to find a way forward. Finally, I felt the Lord tell me to take our ministry school online on a permanent basis, while continuing to offer the in-person option.

I called a special meeting with our BSSM leaders and explained the situation to them. I asked them how long it would take to start an online ministry school. They asked for a couple of days to assess the situation and report back to me. We soon met again. Their research led them to believe it would take approximately six months before we would be ready to accept students. "Yikes," I responded, "we will be bankrupt before then! I need the school up and running in six weeks!" We all just sat there, staring at one another in stunned silence as the minutes ticked away, overwhelmed by the enormity of what we were facing. Finally, our school leader, Steve Moore, said, "We will get back to you!" The next day, they were back in my office. Steve started the meeting by saying, "If all seventy-two of our team members work fourteen hours a day, seven days a week, we can have the online school up and running in six weeks." He continued, "I talked to the entire team and shared how desperate the situation is; *they are all in*, every one of them!" Six weeks later, we enrolled almost eight hundred students! The team saved the day; we transformed the lives of eight hundred students, salvaged all of the team's jobs, and kept BSSM from going broke. But the extreme sacrifice that they and their families made had another powerful side effect: we all bonded relationally in a way I have rarely experienced. We became a band of brothers and sisters. We were more than a great team—we were a family. They are still an amazing team today! In fact, our online BSSM school is now offered in three languages and has grown to over two thousand students.

The BSSM team became forerunners, helping to forge the way forward for the rest of the Bethel staff. Their willingness to suffer for the sake of the greater good set a new standard for our entire organization. The BSSM online miracle story spread like wildfire among our 850 staff members. Morale began to improve dramatically, and soon nearly every department had a similar story. We were rising out of the ash heap of COVID, slugging our way forward day by day, like Green Berets in the Spirit. But, more important, our relationships with Jesus were growing exponentially as, together, we learned to trust Him.

SUFFERING CHANGES OUR PERSPECTIVE

Suffering can change the way we look at things, and whether that change is positive or negative depends on how we respond to it. I first learned that truth early in life. Like so many people today, I experienced a tough childhood. As I shared in the introduction, I lost my dad when I was three years young (he drowned), and, subsequently, I had two very abusive stepfathers who made the lives of my mother, my siblings, and me a living hell. But as fate would have it, I met my childhood sweetheart, Kathy, when she was twelve years old and I was fifteen, and we got engaged a year later (which speaks a lot about our upbringing). Yet we loved one another, and we wanted to be together all the time. Three years later, we found the Lord together and became radical believers. We were married the next year. We were excited to begin our life together after five long years of courting, years full of dreams of a fantastic future. Our first year of marriage was an incredible adventure full of passion, laughter, and fun.

I had a great job managing an auto-repair shop, and Kathy was our bookkeeper. Together, we made enough money to buy a new house and two new cars. We were on our way to fulfilling our dreams. But in the second year of our marriage, life suddenly took a turn for the worse, and soon our lives became almost unbearable. Kathy became pregnant, which was exciting news, but she was so sick that she could hardly get off the couch. While she was fighting her way through the pregnancy, I was carrying tons of responsibility at the auto-repair shop. I managed a team of thirteen people, which proved to be extremely challenging. I worked twelve hours a day, six days a week, and rarely stopped to eat lunch.

THE GRIP OF PANIC

One night, exhausted from a long, hard week of work, I got in the bathtub to relax my tired body, while Kathy lay sick on the sofa. An hour later, I started to get out of the tub but, as I stood up, an *intense* thought hit me: "I am going to die!" Like everyone else in the world, I was no stranger to bad thoughts, but this was different. This thought was so strong that it caused panic to rush through my whole being! My entire body trembled, and my heart pounded out of my chest as my pulse raced uncontrollably. Strength drained from my limbs as I struggled to get out of the tub. I fell back into the water, shouting desperately for Kathy to help me. Eight months pregnant, she labored to get up off the couch and rushed into the bathroom, where I lay helpless, scared, and white as a ghost. I could barely talk, but I managed to mumble something about having a heart attack. She ran into the kitchen and called our family doctor. He relayed a few questions to me through Kathy and concluded that I was having a *panic attack*, not a heart attack. Little did I know that this was the beginning of a three-and-a-half-year journey through hell.

SUFFERING CAN CHANGE THE WAY WE LOOK AT THINGS, AND WHETHER THAT CHANGE IS POSITIVE OR NEGATIVE DEPENDS ON HOW WE RESPOND TO IT.

That first panic attack initiated a constant state of fear in me. Going to work became really tough. It took all the strength I could muster just to get out of bed in the morning. At the shop, throughout the day, high levels of anxiety overwhelmed my soul like waves crashing on the seashore in a violent storm. It was everything I could do just to concentrate on my job. As difficult as the days were, the nights were much worse. The panic attacks continued, turning into endless, tormenting nightmares. Horrible images filled my mind as I imagined terrible things happening to me or envisioned myself doing something dreadful. Although I knew in my heart that these images and thoughts were illusions, they still *felt* so real. I often wondered if I was losing my mind. I couldn't sleep much, and I soaked my sheets with sweat every night.

A year passed without any relief. Kathy and I became so desperate that we quit our jobs and moved up into the mountains to find a slower pace of life. We relocated to Lewiston, California, a town of about nine hundred people way up in the Trinity Alps. Unfortunately, the slower pace of life only served to heighten my awareness of the turmoil going on inside me.

As time passed, the fear intensified, affecting every aspect of my life. I became claustrophobic to such an extent that I had to drive with the windows down so I wouldn't panic. I became reclusive, not wanting to be around people, which eliminated going shopping or to restaurants or to the movies or doing anything else in public.

In the midst of this crazy storm, we were invited to attend a small Assemblies of God church in Weaverville, about fifteen miles from our home. I would sit in the back row and get up to go outside several times during the service to reduce my social anxiety. Yet, somehow, we managed to attend church every Sunday.

TOUGH CIRCUMSTANCES CAN CATALYZE OUR DESTINY

My suffering changed my perspective about life. My dreams were replaced with feelings of hopelessness, and I lost sight of my divine purpose. I knew that the Bible said that "God causes all things to work together for good to those who love God, to those who are called according to His purpose" (Romans 8:28). But, to be honest, it didn't feel true to me. Consequently, I changed the passage in my mind to read, "All good things work out in my favor." This made more sense to me because I couldn't imagine how all things in my life could somehow have a positive outcome. It's just darn hard to be in the midst of a really bad situation and believe that something good—anything remotely defined as good, for that matter—is going to emerge from our suffering. Furthermore, the longer I suffered, the more unrealistic a positive outcome seemed to me. Yet, as I looked deeper into the passage, it got even more ridiculous, because I realized that the Bible was not just saying, "You're going to fully recover from this and be okay." No! It was proclaiming that I actually need this trial, pain, and/or suffering to propel me into my divine

purpose! And the same is true for all of us. The Bible is making an outrageous statement that tough circumstances are actually catalyzing our
destiny. What the heck! How can this be? This marked the beginning
of a gradual new shift in my perspective about suffering.

THE BIBLE MAKES AN OUTRAGEOUS STATEMENT THAT TOUGH CIRCUMSTANCES ARE ACTUALLY CATALYZING OUR DESTINY.

It would be another year and a half before I fully recovered from
my nervous breakdown. But, in the meantime, something incredible
happened. I can still remember the moment as if it were yesterday. The
elders of our little forty-member Assemblies of God church stepped
up front one Sunday morning and introduced our new pastors to the
congregation. "Church, meet your new pastors, Bill and Beni Johnson;
they have been sent here from Bethel Church in Redding, California!"
I sized them up: they were young, and they sort of looked like hippies. I had been hoping for a father, not a hipster! I was still making
judgments in my mind when Bill came to the pulpit to teach. I will
never forget that moment as long as I live. He didn't raise his voice
or act theatrical; he just calmly shared his insights from the Bible. I
had never heard anyone teach with such revelation and depth. It felt
as if the Lord Himself were standing in front of us, delivering the
Word with an anointing that was tangible. I wept through his entire
message, unaware that something else was happening, something
much deeper than hearing a great teaching. It would be years before I
found words to describe it, but I discovered those words in the book of
1 Samuel: *"Now it came about when he [David] had finished speaking to*

Saul, that the soul of Jonathan was knit to the soul of David, and Jonathan loved him as himself" (1 Samuel 18:1). Our families soon became the best of friends and were nearly inseparable for seventeen years. In fact, our families even lived together for six months.

Kathy and I lived a total of twenty years in the mountains of the Trinity Alps. Those were challenging yet wonderful years. We became elders at Mountain Chapel (the church where Bill was pastoring) while raising our four kids and managing nine businesses. Eventually, Bill and Beni were called back to Bethel Church, the same church that had sent them out seventeen years earlier. Two years later, Bill would ask Kathy and me to leave our businesses and join them at Bethel Church to start the school of ministry.

Our suffering during those early years led us to hold onto God desperately in the midst of our crisis, even though we couldn't see any good in it at the time. But, as we did, He led us to enter more fully into His divine purposes for our lives. And, in doing so, He enabled us to *just stand.*

STANDING WITH THOSE WHO SUFFER

There is another kind of suffering that, unfortunately, doesn't seemingly lead to a greater purpose. Sadly, I know this level of suffering firsthand. I was in Taiwan to teach at a conference when the phone rang at three in the morning. I answered the phone drowsily, waking up out of a dead sleep. "Hello," I greeted, at the same time trying to find the light in the hotel room.

"My life is over!" I heard Kathy say through her sobbing.

"What—what the heck? What is going on?" I begged. I was suddenly wide awake!

"I have Parkinson's disease, and my life is over!" she continued, still sobbing.

"Kathy…baby, what happened, honey?" I asked.

She explained, "I just left the neurologist's office. They ran some tests on me, and they informed me that my shaky hand is due to Parkinson's. Kris, my life is over!" We both sobbed together as I tried my best to comfort her through my own shock.

I caught a plane home the next day and entered the nightmare of the suffering of my best friend, my wife, and my lover. On the long journey home, I prayed my guts out, trying to find some way forward. In the midst of my deep grief, the Lord spoke to me. His voice cut through my darkness like a knife. "No one should ever suffer alone," He instructed. Somehow, strangely, His voice brought reassurance to me. I knew that my first priority was to stay close to Kathy, be ready to mourn with her, and learn to not avoid her pain. This was an unexpected twist in our relationship. Aside from when she was ill during her first pregnancy, Kathy had never been sick. She was my rock through two serious nervous breakdowns. I was accustomed to tying off to her in storms. Now, she was the one who needed help, and I was determined to be there for her.

Kathy was diagnosed in 2016, and the struggle remains real. I have worked hard to stay close to her, especially through the really tough days. I have become her coach, her greatest encourager, and her helper in times of need. Kathy loves hunting, fishing, and horses (she has two of them). Parkinson's has made it difficult for her to enjoy some of her hobbies at times due to the stamina, strength, and coordination that is needed for them. Yet she refuses to give up. She spends a couple of hours a day in a massage chair to help keep herself limber, and she uses this opportunity to encourage herself with time with Jesus. She refuses to feel sorry for herself, and she continually reminds herself of all the things she is grateful for. And, the crazy woman still hunts!

In fact, a couple of years ago, she went hunting with a bow and shot a bear at seventy-four yards! It's hard to explain the pure joy of what a feat like that means to a person with a handicap. Right afterward, she FaceTimed me from the hunt, kneeling next to the bear with her bow in hand. I sobbed because I understood that this wasn't so much about killing a bear as it was about refusing to give up, refusing to give in to a disease that threatened to steal her life. In fact, every time she mounts her horse, my eyes well up with tears because I know the sheer risk and struggle of getting on that beast.

A few years ago, Kathy nearly completely stopped going to church. I tried to broach the subject with her, but it was just too painful for her to talk about. One day, she opened up and told me through her tears that she hated being in crowds because she felt like everyone was staring at her shaky hands. I held her close, and we cried together. Then I challenged her to not let her fear of crowds steal her relationship with our church family, whom we have walked with for forty years. "You are a mother to this congregation; they need you!" I exhorted. "If you tell them you have Parkinson's, then they will understand why you have tremors, and they will stop staring at you," I instructed.

A few months later, she agreed to teach at one of our women's gatherings. She spoke on courage, and she used her struggle with Parkinson's as an example of what it's like to get up every day with a life-altering struggle, stare it in the face, and refuse to let it beat you! The women gave her a standing ovation, and she came home with a new lease on life. She had found another reason to live! (More tears were shed by all that night.) Kathy has become a trophy of grace in our family and among our Bethel teams. Her courage in the face of her suffering is a lesson for all of us to never give in and never give up.

BONDING IN BATTLE

Yet there is another dynamic that reigns true in suffering that is rarely talked about: it's the bond that is forged in the fire of distress. We live in a world that runs from pain and avoids suffering at any cost. In our efforts to avoid pain, we squander the opportunity to experience the Master's hand of reassurance and comfort. Paul put it like this: *"That I may know Him and the power of His resurrection and the fellowship of His sufferings*" (Philippians 3:10). The Greek word translated "*fellowship*" here is *koinōnia*, and it means "the share which one has in anything, participation."[12] In other words, we share in Christ's suffering, which means suffering doesn't only bond us to each other, but it also bonds us to the Lord. Whenever we step into the fire with our friends, a fourth Man, the Son of Man, joins us in the furnace. (See Daniel 3:1–27.) If you are looking for Jesus, you'll find Him in a suffering servant, in a terminally ill child, or in a lonely teenager.

The Bible makes a direct connection between suffering and glory, proclaiming:

> *The Spirit Himself testifies with our spirit that we are children of God, and if children, heirs also, heirs of God and fellow heirs with Christ, if indeed we suffer with Him so that we may also be glorified with Him. For I consider that the sufferings of this present time are not worthy to be compared with the glory that is to be revealed to us.*
>
> (Romans 8:16–18)

Did you notice that it doesn't say, "If indeed we suffer *for* Him"? It says, "*suffer **with** Him*"! In other words, we join Him in suffering. What does that mean? It means that wherever there is suffering, Jesus is in the midst of it. He is inviting us to join Him in the fellowship of the suffering of others. It's in the fray that He conducts His Master class of compassion, where we experience the intensity of His love.

WHY ME?

If you find yourself suffering, remember that Jesus is near to you. He is close to the brokenhearted (see Psalm 34:18), and He draws near to the oppressed (see, for example, Psalm 9:9). A divine portal opens up in the heavenly realm when we dare to breach the curtain of suffering, press past the pain of our situation, and hide ourselves in God's holy

---

12. "G2842—koinōnia—Strong's Greek Lexicon (KJV)," Blue Letter Bible, accessed June 10, 2025, https://www.blueletterbible.org/lexicon/g2842/kjv/tr/0-1/.

habitation. He is there for us, caring for us and carrying us through our darkest days. Don't give up! Don't become bitter! Look for Him in your pain; He is there, sitting with you, loving on you, and suffering with you. Soon our suffering will be over, but the bonds we build with God and other believers in these tough times will last forever!

6

IN THE BELLY
OF THE WHALE

Sometimes, we create our own suffering by refusing to obey God and rebelling against His will. The prophet Jonah is the poster child for running from the will of God! Let's review the gist of his story. God sent Jonah to the city of Nineveh to warn the people of a coming calamity—judgment for their sin—but he refused to go. Jonah's rebellion reached a boiling point when he boarded a ship, attempting to sail away from the will of God. So, God sent a terrible storm against the ship, and all the sailors feared for their lives. Although they didn't know the Lord, these sailors had a deep sense that the storm was somehow related to someone on board having disobeyed or offended the gods. In desperation, the men cast lots to see which one of them was guilty, and the lot fell to Jonah. Jonah confessed that he was running from the presence of God because he didn't want to carry out His will. He instructed the men to throw him overboard, and the storm would cease. Reluctantly, the sailors threw him into the sea, and the sea became calm.

This is where the story gets even crazier: a whale (or a *very* large fish) swallowed Jonah up. Jonah lived in that beast for three days while he did a little soul-searching. (I know this story sounds a little fishy, but....) Finally, the whale vomited the dude up on the shore. Jonah made his way to the city and proclaimed God's judgment against the Ninevites. The king, along with the entire city, suddenly repented! Consequently, God relented and withdrew His wrath from the community—to the displeasure of Jonah. (See Jonah 1–3.)

Sometimes, we are desperate to be isolated from the troubles of the world around us, but we are ignorant of the fact that our own disobedience is the very thing that created the storm in which we find ourselves! We cry out to Jesus like the disciples did on the Sea of Galilee—when the Master slept in the stern of the boat during a storm—saying, "Lord, save us!" (See Matthew 8:23–27; see also Mark 4:35–41; Luke 8:22–25.) Yet, unlike the disciples' experience, where the Lord rebuked the storm and calmed the sea, our storm rages on! The truth is, the Lord will calm the Sea of Galilee, but, without our repentance, He will seldom calm the sea of disobedience, rebellion, or sin. In fact, it's not beyond the Lord to cause a storm in our lives and, consequently, for our only remedy to be a whale of a solution.

But wait—there is good news: after Jonah spent three days and nights in the belly of the whale, he had a change of heart. His ultimate obedience not only transformed a wicked city, but it also became a prophetic declaration of the resurrection of Jesus Christ! Check it out. Jesus said:

> *An evil and adulterous generation craves for a sign; and yet no sign will be given to it but the sign of Jonah the prophet; for just as Jonah was three days and three nights in the belly of the sea monster, so will the Son of Man be three days and three nights in the heart of the earth.* (Matthew 12:39–40)

You may have found yourself in the storm of a lifetime, and it may very well *not* be your fault. If your heart is right, and your way is pure, you should have faith that the Lord is going to calm your storm. On the other hand, if you have found yourself in a Jonah storm, the only answer is repentance, obedience, and submission to the will of God. The reality is, there are three reasons for the stormy trials of life. Let's dig a little deeper.

IF YOU HAVE FOUND YOURSELF IN A JONAH STORM, THE ONLY ANSWER IS REPENTANCE, OBEDIENCE, AND SUBMISSION TO THE WILL OF GOD.

FINDING ANSWERS: THE THREE TYPES OF TRIALS

1. TRIALS SENT FROM SATAN

First, there are trials instigated by the devil, which are manifestations of spiritual warfare. Such trials are sent with the intention of undermining or destroying our lives. We must submit to God and *resist* the devil, and he will flee from us. (See James 4:7.) This is the way out of trials rooted in warfare. Warfare is discerned by more than just circumstantial evidence because it often involves a sense of doom, depression, hopelessness, and/or suicidal thoughts. It's also common for a person in a spiritual battle to have nightmares, demonic visitations, and/or other negative spiritual experiences. I wrote an entire book on the subject of spiritual warfare entitled *Spirit Wars: Winning the Invisible Battle Against Sin and the Enemy.*[13] If you think your trials are rooted in warfare, I highly recommend this book.

---

13. Kris Vallotton, *Spirit Wars: Winning the Invisible Battle Against Sin and the Enemy* (Minneapolis, MN: Chosen, 2012).

2. TRIALS CAUSED BY OUR DISOBEDIENCE

The second type of trial is the kind we cause by our own disobedience, sin, and/or encumbrances. We touched on this earlier, but I am personally astounded by the number of Christians who, like Jonah, live life in opposition to the will of God and then wonder why their entire world is one big raging storm! Many of them are claiming the apostle James's promise about trials that test our faith—which we'll address in the next section. They think that somehow their rebellion and subsequent reaping of a whirlwind in life is strengthening their faith. I recently had a conversation with someone that reminded me of this mindset. He says he "loves the Lord," but he lives with his girlfriend in a sexual relationship, and his girlfriend isn't even a Christian. I kindly confronted him, and our conversation went something like this:

"Dude, do you know that living with your girlfriend is called fornication and is sin?"

"Yeah…I know…but the Lord knows my heart."

"Well, if your girlfriend says, 'Live with me,' and the Lord says, 'Don't live with her,' and you do what she tells you to do instead of what He tells you to do, it sounds like you have a new master! I'm not sure she was designed to be a god…maybe you should check her résumé. Because her being all-responsible without being all-powerful might put a strain on your relationship."

"Yes, but I'm not doing what she wants me to do; I'm doing what I want to do."

"Got it! So, you trust yourself more than you trust God…right? Because, you have a god in your own image. Again, being your own god is a full-time endeavor. Remember to call on yourself when you are in trouble, because you are your own higher power!"

Ultimately, if you live in opposition to God's will, you will reap what you sow, because you never really break the law—it only breaks you! Author Gary Chapman introduced us to the five love languages in his book by the same name. But Jesus has a love language that's not in that book: it's called "obedience." Jesus put it like this: *"If you love Me, you will keep My commandments"* (John 14:15). My wife loves it when I serve her; her love language is "acts of service." Jesus loves it when I serve Him, also; but, unlike my wife, He first demands that I obey Him. Jesus is my Friend, my Lover, my Savior, and my Healer. He is my Life, my Teacher, and my Leader. But He is also my *Master*, my *God*, and the only one who deserves 100 percent obedience! He is *always* right! His opinion is rooted in love and bathed in wisdom, and it leads to wholeness.

3. TRIALS SENT FROM GOD

The third kind of trial we face in life is the one sent to us by God. The apostle James has some great insight into these kinds of trials:

Consider it all joy, my brethren, when you encounter various trials, knowing that the testing of your faith produces endurance. And let endurance have its perfect result, so that you may be perfect and complete, lacking in nothing. But if any of you lacks wisdom, let him ask of God, who gives to all generously and without reproach, and it will be given to him. But he must ask in faith without any doubting, for the one who doubts is like the surf of the sea, driven and tossed by the wind. For that man ought not to expect that he will receive anything from the Lord, being a double-minded man, unstable in all his ways.

(James 1:2–8)

James speaks of trials that "test our faith." These trials are meant to strengthen our faith, deepen our resolve, and build our character. The only way through trials sent by God is to go deeper with Him! Since these trials are primarily meant to test our faith, this means that the goal of our response to difficult circumstances is to trust God with the outcome. This often feels high risk and, at times, not rational or not even possible. Sometimes, the things the Lord requires us to do to actualize our faith can feel (or even be) ridiculous. Consider the story of Joshua taking the city of Jericho by having his army walk around the city for seven days and then shout so that the walls would fall down. (See Joshua 6:1–21.) Or how about the story of Gideon, whom the Lord commanded to reduce his army to three hundred men against an army that numbered the sands of the sea? The battle plan: yeah, about that.... God instructed Gideon to get some jars, trumpets, and torches. Then Gideon commanded his three hundred fighting men to blow the trumpets, break the jars, and light the torches while shouting, *"For the LORD and for Gideon!"* Yep, that was the battle plan. Oh, by the way, it worked! (See Joshua 7.)

NAVIGATING A STORM

When you consider the three types of trials, where do you see the greatest challenge in your life? Are your trials rooted, as Jonah's were, in your disobedience, your running from the will of God? Or perhaps you are in the midst of demonic warfare, and you just realized that your strategy for victory needs an overhaul. Or could it be that the Lord has you in His boot camp, and you are learning to trust Him?

Maybe you are saying to yourself, "I have no idea what the source of my trials are!" You might be in the eye of a storm, trying to understand the way to safety. Sometimes, it's hard to find your way out if you are deeply invested in your own disobedience. Have you found yourself entrenched in immorality or impurity, bitterness or hatred, or something else that is pulling you away from God—but you refuse to admit that you are wrong? Let me tell you: humility is the only way forward! Furthermore, the writer of Hebrews said, *"Let us also lay aside every encumbrance and the sin which so easily entangles us, and let us run with endurance the race that is set before us"* (Hebrews 12:1). As I pointed out in an earlier chapter, sin entangles us, but so do other types of encumbrances. Sin probably doesn't need much explanation, because it means disobedience to God, doing evil, and/or living for yourself. But encumbrances are different: remember that the Greek word translated as *"encumbrance"* is *ogkos*, which means "bulk," "mass," or "weight," as in a heavy load.

Perhaps your encumbrance has to do with a lack of purpose. So many people are dragging around a ball and chain tied around their waist as they do life. They hate their job or their living situation, and they constantly complain about it, but it's the only life they know. These stuck people remind me of a situation my wife and I dealt with many years ago. When we owned our auto-parts store, we had a customer whose name was Henry. Henry was a Christian, and he was in the automotive field, so he was in our parts house several times a day for years. Henry's business was his encumbrance. He hated being in the automotive field and literally complained about *everything*! In fact, his negativity was so toxic that our countermen would run for the bathroom when they saw him coming through the door. Of course, this gave Henry something else to complain about (not that he actually needed any more evidence that the entire world was against him).

I became so sick of Henry's perpetual griping that I finally decided to help him find a way out of his situation. I sat with him for hours over the course of a week and challenged him to find an occupation that inspired him. After a while, it became clear that Henry had aspirations for greater things, but he was terrified of the unknown! His life was miserable but predictable. He ultimately chose the predictable cycle of an unhappy life because his fear of change was greater than the pain of redundancy that he was enduring.

Sadly, Henry was a perfect example of a life encumbered by a lack of purpose and imprisoned by anxieties. He was shackled to his dread and confined by an invisible but powerful taskmaster that taunted him into submission. Henry was a powerless Christian who died a miserable, unhappy, unfulfilled man; and, as you might have guessed, there weren't many people at his funeral.

START OVER NOW

Jesus told the following story, pointing the way for us to return to God by obeying Him and fulfilling His purpose for our life:

"A man had two sons, and he came to the first and said, 'Son, go work today in the vineyard.' And he answered, 'I will not'; but afterward he regretted it and went. The man came to the second and said the same thing; and he answered, 'I will, sir'; but he did not go. Which of the two did the will of his father? They [the religious leaders] *said, "The first." Jesus said to them, "Truly I say to you that the tax collectors and prostitutes will get into the kingdom of God before you."*

(Matthew 21:28–31)

You may be like Jonah, or like the first son in the story above. If so, you are what I call a "spiritually late adopter"! In fact, Jesus used the examples of the prostitute and the tax collector—who were considered the scum of the earth at that time, the least likely to succeed—to illustrate the kind of people who say *no* to God at first but later change their minds and obey. As Jesus indicated, in a race, it's not the first mile that counts; it's the last!

Many of us may not have a Jonah life, in which we are sailing away from the will of God, but we may be having a Jonah *experience* in which, although we are called to something great, we have settled for something that is somewhat less risky. In Jonah's case, his reluctance to radically obey God was likely rooted in his fear of looking like a false prophet and being rejected by the people. He knew that God was loving and compassionate; therefore, he understood that if he prophesied judgment against Nineveh, and the city repented, God would change his mind, and Jonah would have egg on his face. Actually, the very thing that Jonah feared took place just as he had imagined. When God withdrew His wrath from Nineveh, Jonah sulked like a spoiled child! He was angry that God didn't kill the one hundred and twenty thousand inhabitants of the city to vindicate him. (See Jonah 4.) Jonah was a gifted prophet, but he was a self-centered, self-absorbed, miserable person.

If you've been running from God—even in the smallest of ways—know this: He's still waiting to welcome you back, arms wide open. But love isn't just something we say; it's something we live. So let's not just say, "Lord, I will." Let's follow through and show Him with our choices, not just our words.

IF YOU'VE BEEN RUNNING FROM GOD— EVEN IN THE SMALLEST OF WAYS—KNOW THIS: HE'S STILL WAITING TO WELCOME YOU BACK, ARMS WIDE OPEN.

LIFE IS MEANT TO BE EXCITING

Life in Jesus is meant to be an exciting adventure! It's full of ups and downs, twists and turns, but it's *never boring*! Living to protect our reputation or being overly concerned about the opinions of others will steal our joy and undermine our divine assignment. Our life in Christ is meant to be spent serving others, helping other people to succeed, and using our gifts for the betterment of the world around us. There's nothing wrong with our having nice things and prospering, as long as our primary, core motivation is to serve the Lord by helping others to succeed in life, too.

There's a great account of John D. Rockefeller's life by Waylon Bailey that illustrates this.[14] Bailey describes how, at the height of the industrial revolution, Rockefeller was a young man who emerged as a titan of enterprise. Born in 1839, he amassed incredible wealth early on. He became a millionaire in his thirties, which, in the economic climate of the 1870s, was like holding a small nation's treasury. By forty, he was steering Standard Oil, a corporation so vast it controlled about

---

14. This account of John D. Rockefeller was adapted and expanded from Waylon Bailey, "The Remarkable Story of John D. Rockefeller, Sr.," First Baptist Church Covington, https://fbccov.org/the-remarkable-story-of-john-d-rockefeller-sr/. Courtesy of Waylon Bailey.

90 percent of America's oil. Eventually, he became the world's only billionaire at the time, his net worth reaching a modern equivalent of $336 billion—making him one of the wealthiest individuals the world has ever known.

Yet, despite all his wealth, Rockefeller's body began to crumble in ways no money could mend. By his mid-fifties, the most powerful man in business could barely eat more than dry crackers, and sleep eluded him night after night. His health spiraled, and doctors gave him a grim prognosis: he likely wouldn't survive another year.

Faced with his own mortality, Rockefeller underwent a transformation that had little to do with finance. Realizing he couldn't take a dime with him, he began giving his money away—lavishly and intentionally. He invested millions into churches, funded universities from Chicago to the Philippines, and launched medical institutions, including what is now Rockefeller University. Through his foundation, breakthroughs like penicillin and the fight against yellow fever were made possible.

Then, something remarkable happened. As he gave, healing followed. His stomach condition lifted, his sleep returned, and his soul awakened. In a personal journal entry, he reflected: "God taught me that everything belongs to Him, and I am merely a conduit to carry out His will. My life has been one long, happy holiday since then; full of work and play, I let go of my worries along the road, and God was wonderful to me every day."[15]

Rockefeller didn't die the next year. In fact, he lived more than four decades longer—passing away at the age of ninety-seven—not just as a man of wealth, but as a man who had learned to live well.

WHALE TALES

It may sound crazy, but living a comfortable life will kill you! Living for yourself is a really bad plan that will ultimately cost you your life

15. Ralph Burden, "John D. Rockefeller and the Power of Generosity," Real Life Stories, https://www.reallifestories.org/stories/john-d-rockefeller-and-the-power-of-generosity/.

because you can't keep what was meant to be given away. On the other hand, living as a radical believer who is selfless, generous, humble, and obedient will fill your days with purpose and gratification. Ironically, in 1965, in the midst of the sexual revolution, the Rolling Stones sang a song about their inability to find satisfaction in their lives. The song is called, "(I Can't Get No) Satisfaction." Unfortunately, that old rock-and-roll hit is the theme song for way too many Christians.

King David was a man after God's own heart, but even he had seasons in his life when he was self-absorbed and reckless. One spring, during the time when kings go out to war, David stayed home and sipped some suds on the roof of his palace. That's when David saw Bathsheba, who was married to Uriah, one of David's thirty-three mighty men. But David was in an arrogant stupor that spring and, consequently, decided to take Bathsheba to bed. She became pregnant, and David ultimately murdered Uriah because he didn't have the character or the courage to own up to his colossal failure! (See 2 Samuel 11.) The Hebrew name *Uriah* means "God is my flame,"[16] and David certainly extinguished his own fire for God that year, and thus paid a heavy price for it. You would think that going to war would be exponentially more dangerous than staying home in a fortified palace. Yet, the truth is, when God sends us to war, He protects us! Therefore, the safest place to be—the place where we can continually stand strong—is in the will of God!

---

16. "H223–ûrîyâ—Strong's Hebrew Lexicon (KJV)," Blue Letter Bible, accessed June 25, 2025, https://www.blueletterbible.org/lexicon/h223/kjv/wlc/0-1/.

7

FAILING SUCCESSFULLY

You have heard it said, "If life gives you lemons, make lemonade." But what do you do when you're pursuing nobility, yet you're sitting in a pile of crap, and you know it's your fault? How do you go on when you have defecated all over yourself, and the stink of your life has isolated you? Rather than letting the dung destroy us, we need to learn how to turn it into fertilizer that grows us. T.D. Jakes has pointed out, "Most of us think we are being buried when in fact we are only being planted!"[17]

This point was driven home to me in a powerful way. I was once at a men's conference where the men were encouraged to confess to the group anything that was keeping them from being fully alive and completely free. Some of the confessions were truly heartbreaking, but the one that moved me the most was from a man who was an ex-convict. He was riddled with shame as he stood up and confessed, "I spent

17. T.D. Jakes, "You're Not Being Buried, You're Being Planted," TBN YouTube channel, 17:04, https://youtu.be/VzNdV-wL5V0?si=w-J0XAgOu4ZNOA6s&t=1024.

years in prison for killing a child while driving drunk." The man was sobbing as he recounted his demise, the devastation he had caused the child's entire family, and the shame he had brought on his own family. A few minutes passed as the intensity in the group grew. Then, unexpectedly, his adult son stood up and rushed to his father's side. He wrapped his arms around his dad and declared, "Dad, I love you! Dad, I forgive you. Dad, you are forgiven!"

Unfortunately, the world is filled with people who have done horrific and/or detestable things—some on purpose and others by accident, which, nonetheless, were destructive. So many marriages, families, and individuals have been destroyed by drug or alcohol addiction, theft, unfaithfulness, rape, molestation, murder…the list could go on and on. Society is full of people who have failed miserably—and thus were many of us! The question is, "Can they ever recover? Can we?" In other words, is there any way forward for those of us who have had a colossal failure?

The reality of failure is much more complex than a theological dissertation might convey. Extending someone mercy is often far easier than trusting their repentance. We want to forgive people (including ourselves) who have had a massive failure in their lives, but are they and we prone to fail in the same way again? Furthermore, our society has a sin-grading system that does have some sense of justice instilled in it, although it seems skewed at times. For instance, those who have committed sexual abuse or sexual assault have to register as a sex offender for the rest of their lives. Every time they move to a different residence, they have to notify the authorities of their new location. On the other hand, someone who murders an entire family (which may include children) and fulfills their prison sentence is free to live without legal oversight or restrictions.

These situations bear introspection: What is the purpose of our prison system? Does spending time in prison reform a person? Does punishment create justice? How do you measure the value of a life? Is there a way to ensure that a person won't repeat their crime? What does eternity look like for those who steal, kill, and destroy the lives of others? Can the surviving victims of hideous crimes ever truly recover? These questions have been debated for centuries in the highest courts of our land and among America's smartest Supreme Court justices; they have been discussed in seminaries by our brightest theologians and considered deeply by the most notable psychiatrists and psychologists of our time. Yet there remain many unanswered questions and differences of opinion among the experts. Therefore, it's hard to imagine that we will answer these challenging, life-changing questions in one chapter of a book. However, it's important to look a little closer at the subject to see if we can gain a few insights into this topic that can help us, our loved ones, and even those who may have hurt us.

THOSE WHO FAILED SUCCESSFULLY

A while back, Paul Manwaring made a huge impact on my heart regarding this topic. Paul is an Englishman who came to Redding a couple of decades ago with his wife, Sue, to attend Bethel School of Supernatural Ministry. He soon became one of our most respected pastors at Bethel Church. Paul was a former governor of a juvenile prison in the United Kingdom (UK). He used to stand in front of his young prisoners and rip out every page of the Bible that was written by a murderer. He tore out the first five books of the Bible, which were written by Moses. Next came the psalms that King David penned. He moved on to the New Testament and began ripping out Romans, 1 and 2 Corinthians, Galatians, Ephesians.... He continued until he had removed all thirteen books written by the apostle Paul, which left only *half* the books of the New Testament! As he ripped out each page of the Bible, he would yell, "Written by a murderer!" [RIP!] "Written by a *murderer!*" [RIP!] "*Written by a murderer!*" [RIP, RIP, RIP, RIP!]

What an incredibly brilliant way to illustrate that people who were the dung of society became holy people who were given the absolute privilege and responsibility of penning the very words of God in the most sacred book ever written. Of course, we could add other books of the Bible that were written by people who failed, such as the apostle Peter, who denied Christ three times after he was warned by Jesus a few hours earlier that he would do just that. [RIP, RIP!] There is also Solomon, who started well but finished horribly—there go three more books from the Holy Bible. [RIP, RIP, RIP!] I hope the point is clear by now: God can and often does transform people from evil creeps into godly saints.

> PEOPLE WHO WERE THE DUNG OF SOCIETY BECAME HOLY PEOPLE WHO WERE GIVEN THE ABSOLUTE PRIVILEGE AND RESPONSIBILITY OF PENNING THE VERY WORDS OF GOD IN THE MOST SACRED BOOK EVER WRITTEN.

FALLEN SAINTS

The toughest situations to understand are when people of God—saints, who have been born-again and have a new nature—commit serious atrocities against others. The most well-known failures in the body of Christ are leaders, people whom we follow, learn from, and respect! In fact, there seems to be a growing list of leaders who have crashed and burned, leaving behind so much carnage that it's mind-boggling.

The Lord is cleaning house and exposing the evil in His church that, in many cases, has been going on for decades. The apostle Peter wrote, *"For it is time for judgment to begin with the household of God; and if it begins with us first, what will be the outcome for those who do not obey the gospel of God?"* (1 Peter 4:17). The Greek word translated as *"time"* in this passage is *kairos,* which can mean "opportune time," "proper time," "the right time," and "season."[18]

The concept of "kairos" judgments was never more evident than it was in the early church when God killed Ananias and Sapphira for lying about a property deal. The church was young and innocent, and the Lord wanted the foundation of His spiritual community to be established on honesty, honor, and generosity. People in the congregation were giving everything they had—laying down their lives for the poor and needy among them by selling their properties and giving *all* the proceeds to the cause. Their extreme generosity became a spiritual standard that separated those who were half-hearted, double-minded, or lukewarm from those who were on fire, all-in, and passionate. Ananias and Sapphira got caught up in the passion of the moment. They sold their property, but they gave only a portion of the proceeds to the cause. Then they lied about their half-hearted financial transaction so that they could appear as if they, too, were surrendered lovers of God. Both of them died for their dishonesty! (See Acts 5:1–11.) But I would like to point out that their lying, in itself, wasn't what killed them; it was *when* they lied! If that was God's standard for everyday life in the church, I'm not sure who would still be alive! But they were living in a kairos time when God was building a pure church, and He was not going to allow double-minded, half-hearted people to pollute the foundation of His holy believers. A similar kairos season appears to be upon us, when God Himself is purifying His people.

WARFARE AND JUDGMENT

The apostle Paul has incredible insights into the dynamic that warfare plays in the judgment of God. In 2 Corinthians, he opened up this

---

18. "G2540–kairos–Strong's Greek Lexicon (KJV)," Blue Letter Bible, accessed June 17, 2025, https://www.blueletterbible.org/lexicon/g2540/kjv/tr/0-1/; "2540. Kairos," Bible Lexicon, Bible Hub, accessed June 17, 2025, https://biblehub.com/greek/2540.htm.

subject by talking about his authority among the Corinthians, a church he had planted and for which he was the spiritual father:

> *Now I, Paul, myself urge you by the meekness and gentleness of Christ—I who am meek when face to face with you, but bold toward you when absent! I ask that when I am present I need not be bold with the confidence with which I propose to be courageous against some, who regard us as if we walked according to the flesh.*
>
> (2 Corinthians 10:1–2)

Paul stated that there were people in the congregation who were accusing him of walking in the flesh. The indictment was that his bold correction to them wasn't rooted in the Spirit of God. His rebuttal to them is epic:

> *For though we walk in the flesh, we do not war according to the flesh, for the weapons of our warfare are not of the flesh, but divinely powerful for the destruction of fortresses. We are destroying speculations and every lofty thing raised up against the knowledge of God, and we are taking every thought captive to the obedience of Christ, and we are ready to punish all disobedience, whenever your obedience is complete.*
>
> (2 Corinthians 10:3–6)

Contextually, Paul was talking about the demonic warfare that was affecting the Corinthian church, which had been saved out of Greek mythology. You can imagine the challenges this first-century congregation was facing as they navigated the debauchery of their former life and their journey into righteous nobility as children of God. Paul pointed out that his correction in their lives was actually spiritual warfare! The overarching connotation is that their lifestyle of disobedience was not simply an act of their free will but part of a demonic scheme to destroy them. His words of direction, instruction, rebuke, and correction were spiritual bombs—powerful weapons flowing from his words to free them from the chains of satanic bondage. Yet there were those in the congregation who were participating in *"fruitless deeds of darkness"*

(Ephesians 5:11 NIV) willingly, not under demonic compulsion. Their willful disobedience had to be punished. But Paul was unwilling to decree judgment against them until those who were in the midst of a spiritual battle that was waging war against their souls found freedom and walked in a manner worthy of their calling!

There is so much wisdom in Paul's dealings with this young church as he led them into maturity in Jesus. He made them aware that there were people who willfully preyed on the body of Christ, and that such people had to be dealt with while grace was being given to those who were still working out their salvation and whose disobedience was rooted in warfare and immaturity. Practically speaking, this is a fine line that requires extreme discernment, patience, and wisdom.

WHEAT AND TARES

This reminds me of the parable Jesus told about the wheat and the tares, which grow together in the field. Wheat and tares look so similar before they come to maturity that it's hard to tell them apart. But when the wheat comes of age, the fruit manifests at the end of the stalk, which, consequently, causes them to lean over from the weight of the crop. Jesus warned us about pulling up the tares too soon and accidently destroying some immature wheat. (See Matthew 13:24–30.) There are so many biblical metaphors and examples that explain this principle of discerning good from evil and the challenge it presents in our everyday walk with God: wolves disguised in sheep's clothing (see Matthew 7:15), the devil masquerading as an angel of light (2 Corinthians 11:14), wheat and tares growing together until harvesttime, murder-minded Sauls becoming passionate, Jesus-following Pauls (see Acts 9:1–19)... the list could go on and on! There are many people who are in the process of spiritual growth but haven't yet come to maturity. Conversely, there are people whose motives are evil and whose ways are destructive to God's purposes. If these harmful people are not confronted, they will wreak havoc on the body of Christ by exploiting the mercy and kindness of believers and preying on the vulnerabilities of the weak, young, and unlearned.

Furthermore, it's important to point out that tares are not immature wheat—they are weeds that are competing for the nourishment of the soil but will *never* produce fruit!

WHENEVER GOD INITIATES AN EPOCH TIME OF JUDGMENT, HE ALSO PROVIDES EXTREME GRACE THAT GIVES US THE POWER TO CHANGE AND GROW IN HOLINESS.

GRACE TO CHANGE

Whenever God initiates an epoch time of judgment, He also provides extreme grace that gives us the power to change and grow in holiness. I recently experienced this in my own life. I grew up in the streets of San Francisco, the Bay Area of California, and, as I mentioned previously, I worked in the blue-collar, auto-repair industry. Vulgar language was a big part of our culture, and thus swearing became habitual in my life. When I got saved at eighteen, much of my vulgarity fell away, especially the language around sexuality and women. But I still cussed privately, and, honestly, I never felt convicted about it. Then, during the spring of 2022, I woke up in the middle of the night, and it felt like the Lord was waiting to greet me. As I gathered myself and was about to make my way to the restroom, the Lord said, *No more cussing!* That was it—just three short words, and grace to change was instantly released to me. Of course, I had to embrace the correction and manage my tongue, but the change was immediate. As of this writing, it's been several years, and I have rarely fallen in this area!

VICTIMS RESTORED

Although God forgives us and gives us grace to change, there are often victims of our sinful pasts and our unholy lifestyles. The victims of any assault should be protected, heard, and helped into wholeness by church leadership and the rest of the body of Christ. Also, a high standard of holiness needs to be expected, inspected, and modeled, especially by church leaders on any staff or team. Furthermore, there needs to be strong, real, authentic accountability for everyone, but particularly for leaders. This necessitates having a method of reporting unwanted, unholy, and/or unrighteous behavior in a way that doesn't create backlash for the alleged victim, no matter who the alleged perpetrator is. Victims must always be our first priority!

Too often, bad behavior—especially by those in power—goes unreported and, therefore, is not confronted for years because the victims fear the repercussions of their bosses, leaders, and/or organizations. Will they lose their jobs, find their promotions undermined, or be viewed as problem employees? Will anyone believe them, especially if they are reporting the poor behavior of a popular leader? Such fears are real and should be taken seriously. Of course, we shouldn't rush to judgment, because a person should be deemed innocent until they are proven guilty. It's also not uncommon for there sometimes to be misunderstandings and/or miscommunications between people that lead them to wrong conclusions or to misjudging a person's motives. Yet, the truth is, there are many victims of sexual abuse who have stepped forward, only to be silenced by the leadership of their organization. We have to build a culture that embraces a practical system of accountability that investigates and confronts any and all forms of abuse and lays out a process of wholeness for everyone involved. This may include terminating a leader or leaders and employing law enforcement and the justice system to allow the courts to determine the proper outcome of certain violations. But we also must *never* lose sight of God's power to heal and restore anyone and everyone to wholeness—whether victim or perpetrator.

DEALING WITH THE VICTIMIZER

There is a powerful decree in the book of Isaiah that is a piece of the "Messiah Mandate" that Jesus quoted when He began His public ministry. It reads: *"The Spirit of the Lord* GOD *is upon me, because the* LORD *has anointed me to bring good news to the afflicted; He has sent me to bind up the brokenhearted, to proclaim liberty to captives and freedom to prisoners"* (Isaiah 61:1). It's important to understand that Jesus is liberating captives—*victims* who have been accosted by evil. But He is also freeing prisoners—people who have *victimized* others and are, therefore, incarcerated. The victimizer must be given a path of repentance and restoration. This is a bedrock truth of the kingdom of God!

The gospel isn't just for the righteous; it's also for the unrighteous, the unholy, the sinner who commits the audacious sin—the socially unacceptable transgression. Frankly, this is where the crowd goes crazy! We love the story of the woman who was caught in adultery and accused by the crowd but forgiven by Jesus. (See John 8:1–11.) But we often don't read the story in its context. She was an "adulteress" (as opposed to a "fornicator," who would have had sex outside of marriage as a single person). Either she was married and having sex with a married man who wasn't her husband, or she was having sex with an unmarried man outside of her marriage. Whatever the case, the affair must have gone on long enough that the religious leaders, who caught the woman in the act of adultery in sort of a sting operation, knew where to find the adulterous couple when they wanted to put Jesus to the test.

Now, let's suppose that you are the man who is married to the adulterous woman, and you have a couple of kids; it's your wife who just got caught having sex with your neighbor. In this case, you and the children are the victims, and your wife is the victimizer (along with the guy she was having sex with)! The crowd wants to bring justice by stoning her to death. Jesus doesn't suggest a lesser punishment or marriage counseling; instead, He instructs the mob to let the person who has no sin start the stoning, and then the others can join in. In light of the standard Jesus set to bring judgment to the situation, the crowd begins to peel off one by one as they realize that their sin also deserves judgment. Notice that Jesus didn't say, "Let the one who's never committed adultery throw the first stone!" He said, "Let any one of you who is without sin be the first to throw a stone."

You see, the crowd has a grading system for sin. It's called relative righteousness, and it goes something like this: "I have never committed sin at the level of your sin; therefore, I am more righteous than you are. So, my anger toward you, the violator, is justified. Furthermore, I will demonstrate my righteousness by letting everyone know that I'm vigilant in my protection of the victim. And, finally, I don't view myself as a villain when I sin, because I see my own sin as a victimless crime."

It's important to point out here that Jesus told the woman in the story that He didn't condemn her. Then He left her with this exhortation: "Go your way. From now on sin *no more*" (John 8:11 NASB77). In other words, telling her to never sin again isn't condemnation; it's "*speaking the truth in love*" (Ephesians 4:15). But you can't tell the truth with stones in your hands and call it love! Mercy is very important, but it's truth that sets us free. (See John 8:32.)

JUDGMENT AND MERCY

I'm moved by how loving yet authentic God is with His people who fail. For instance, God said that David was "*a man after His own heart*" (see 1 Samuel 13:14; Acts 13:22), but He includes in the Bible the story of David's adulterous relationship with Bathsheba (which may even have been a rape), and the murder of her husband, Uriah (see 2 Samuel 11). Conversely, after exposing David's incredible failure through the prophet Nathan, and having David and Bathsheba walk out the loss of their first child, the Lord unapologetically blessed them with another son, named Solomon. Out of all David's children, Solomon was called by God to inherit the kingship of Israel from David. God is not ashamed of His fallen friends, and He doesn't do "guilt by association"!

The Bible has a lot to say about the restoration of people. The apostle Paul put it like this: *"Brethren, even if anyone is caught in any trespass, you who are spiritual, restore such a one in a spirit of gentleness; each one looking to yourself, so that you too will not be tempted"* (Galatians 6:1). Spiritual people restore others with humility, knowing their own vulnerabilities. All of us have experienced the power of temptation and the war that often rages against our souls as we resist the lure of its enticement. The Bible says that Jesus was *"tempted in **every way**,"* yet He did not sin. (See Hebrews 4:15 NIV.) It's become common for Christians to call for justice as if they themselves live in a war-free zone, absent of any conflict in their souls. It's only by the grace of God that righteousness is accessible and obtainable by any of us.

A CULTURE OF JUDGMENT

The process of restoration in our lives begins with the confession of our sin to one another. The apostle John expressed it best: *"If we say that we have no sin, we are deceiving ourselves and the truth is not in us. If we confess our sins, He is faithful and righteous to forgive us our sins and to cleanse us from all unrighteousness"* (1 John 1:8–9). The "cleansing from all unrighteousness" comes through the power of God, which purifies our hearts and transforms our lives! But, again, this process begins with confession. If we create a self-righteous, "stoning" culture in which, when people (including leaders) confess their sin, their confession is met with judgment instead of mercy, not many people will have the courage to confess. This will ultimately result in a dysfunctional ecosystem of hidden sin, tons of shame, and virtueless leadership. Self-righteousness opens the door to arrogance in our lives, which is like making a deal with the devil! Look at the discourse that Jesus had with His most trusted leaders:

> Jesus said to them, "You will all fall away, because it is written, 'I will strike down the shepherd, and the sheep shall be scattered.'" …But Peter said to Him, "Even though all may fall away, yet I will not." And Jesus said to him, "Truly I say to you, that this very night, before a rooster crows twice, you yourself will deny Me three times." But Peter kept saying insistently, "Even if I have to die with You, I will not deny You!" And they all were saying the same thing also.
>
> (Mark 14:27, 29–31)

The "Peter syndrome" is alive and well today! Once more, the arrogance of self-righteousness blinds us to our own vulnerabilities as we view ourselves as more spiritual, righteous, or successful than others. Our inner decrees are often Peterish, going something like this: "Other Christians may all fall away, but I certainly never would," or, "You must be referring to those other guys, because I am better than that!"

In the above passage, Jesus gave us insight into the demonic strategies that are at war against the church: "Strike down the shepherd and scatter the sheep." The sheep face temptation, for sure, but not at the same level that the shepherds do. Leaders are at the spear point of the spiritual battle, both personally and corporately. It's imperative that we pray for our leaders.

RISING FROM THE ASHES

The good news is that Peter failed successfully! He denied Christ three times and left the courtyard in utter shame. But, a little while later, he became the most prominent leader of the early church. (See, for example, Mark 14:66–72.) Peter's life is one of the most inspiring stories in the entire Bible. But the untold and often-overlooked dynamic at work in the early church is the believers' ability to recover from disappointment and failure. The other disciples chose to follow Peter despite his boastful arrogance, his accusations against them, and his repeated failures. His failures continued long after his denial of Christ. In fact, many years later, the apostle Paul had to rebuke Peter publicly for his ethnic hypocrisy. (See Galatians 2:11–14.) Yet Peter had an incredible propensity to recover, despite his many shortcomings, missteps, and failures.

THE UNTOLD AND OFTEN-OVERLOOKED
DYNAMIC AT WORK IN THE EARLY
CHURCH IS THE BELIEVERS' ABILITY
TO RECOVER FROM DISAPPOINTMENT
AND FAILURE.

Judas also denied Christ by selling Him out for thirty pieces of silver. His story stands in such stark contrast to Peter's. When Judas realized the gravity of his sin, he went out and hanged himself. (See Matthew 27:3–5.) Can you imagine what his testimony could have been like if he had accepted and experienced the gospel that he had been preaching for those three and a half years? What a wasted talent! What a terrible eternity.

RESTORATION FOR THE FALLEN AND BROKEN

A large piece of Peter's recovery came from that first-century culture of forgiveness and restoration. God is on the move again—rebuilding the same culture of restoration in His church today. Maybe you're part of that redemptive work yourself, helping to lift the fallen and restore the broken to their rightful place. Bethel Church, where I minister, is a house of restoration, healing, and miracles. With our whole heart, we believe that "nothing is impossible with God" (see, for example, Mark

10:27), which attracts thousands of people every year, from all over the world, who need a miracle. Therefore, we find hundreds of broken people, in the worst season of their lives and desperate for a touch from Jesus, visiting on any given week. It's common to find broken and fallen leaders looking for restoration because part of our mandate is the restoration and recovery of the fallen. Furthermore, we reach out to the homeless and the helpless, ministering to them throughout the week. Many of them are mentally ill and/or drug addicted.

This has been Bethel's call for decades. In fact, during the Jesus Movement, some of the elders at Bethel insisted that the "long-haired hippies and the girls in miniskirts" not be allowed in church. But pastor Earl Johnson (Bill Johnson's father) stood against those elders. They left and planted a different church, while Bethel continued to welcome people in all stages of life and spiritual growth.

Our congregation is accustomed to having sinners and saints in fellowship together. In fact, our people are well-equipped to minister to others no matter their condition. Our church is filled with radical believers who call Bethel home and are equipped by the fivefold ministry for the work of service. They are not afraid to dirty their hands with the souls of hurting people. In fact, more than eight hundred of them serve in the Healing Rooms every Saturday—healing the sick, the broken, the demonized, and the mentality ill.

I've been excited to see the same thing happening in many other churches and organizations, as God continues to restore those whose lives are shattered and who are struggling to find hope after an incident—or even a lifetime—of failure. In what ways has God restored you? How have you helped others to be restored and set free?

FAILURE ISN'T FINAL

Maybe, as you read this chapter, you feel stuck in failure mode. What should you do? Or maybe you are close to someone who has had a major failure in their life, and you wonder how to relate to an individual who has blown up their life on purpose, not to mention has produced massive fallout, leaving a trail of tears in their wake from the destruction their sin has caused others.

I encourage you to revisit the pathway to forgiveness and restoration we've walked through in this chapter. Don't go it alone—seek out a trusted leader, a wise advisor, or a mature friend who will tell you the truth in love. Surround yourself with a community of believers who will extend grace and hold you accountable with compassion. You may have failed, but failure doesn't have to be final.

No matter what the situation, remember this: nobody has fallen so far that God can't reach them, or sinned so ruthlessly that they can't be forgiven. *No one!* So, never give up on yourself or others—because Jesus certainly doesn't!

8

WHAT TO DO WHEN YOUR GIRLFRIEND TIES YOU UP: LESSONS FROM THE LIFE OF SAMSON

Samson was an Old Testament superhero. He had supernatural physical strength—similar to the fictional character the Hulk—yet he had a covenant with God. His exploits were otherworldly because he understood that his physical, supernatural capability was a manifestation of this covenant, rooted in his Nazarite vow and demonstrated by the simple obedience of never cutting his hair. (See Judges 13:2–5; Numbers 6:1–8.)

Samson was a warrior, a one-man wrecking crew. In his day, the Philistines were the archenemy of the Israelites. In one exploit alone, Samson took the jawbone of a donkey and killed a thousand Philistine soldiers with it. (See Judges 15:14–16.) Consequently, Samson became public enemy number one on the Philistines' most-wanted list. The Philistine army stalked him like a wild animal, but every time they cornered him, he destroyed them.

On Samson's way to Gaza, a Philistine stronghold that Samson was sent to destroy, he stopped at a brothel and had sex with a harlot. The Philistines found out that he was there and surrounded the place, thinking they had trapped him at the city gate. But, at midnight, Samson *"took hold of the doors of the city gate and the two posts and pulled them up along with the bars; then he put them on his shoulders and carried them up to the top of the mountain which is opposite Hebron."* (See Judges 16:1–3.)

Eventually, the Philistines realized that Samson's weakness was loose women. So, they devised a plan to discover the secret of his strength. They found a beautiful gold digger named Delilah and paid her a ton of cash to seduce Samson into divulging the mystery of his supernatural ability. Samson's intense passion for Delilah blinded him to her very obvious demonic manipulation and undermined his divine call to destroy the works of the enemy.

On several occasions, Delilah tried to seduce Samson to discover the key to his great power. But he toyed with her, telling her that his strength would be nullified if she tied him up in specific ways. Twice she tied him up as he professed and then yelled, *"The Philistines are upon you, Samson!"* (Judges 16:9, 12). Both times, he snapped the ropes effortlessly. But Delilah was persistent, and she continued to manipulate him night after night. Finally, she wore him out, and he revealed that the truth of his strength lay in his covenant with God, predicated, as I shared earlier, on his Nazarite vow and demonstrated by his never cutting his hair. So, Delilah cut his hair while he slept. When he woke up, his supernatural strength was gone. Consequently, the Philistine soldiers tied him up, gouged out his eyes, and ultimately led him to his death. (See Judges 16:15–30; for the full account of Samson's amazing story, read Judges 13–16.)

Samson's life was a contradiction of dedication to God through his Nazarite vow and deep sexual brokenness, in which he literally became a slave to his sex drive. He had no discernment in the presence of beautiful women who seduced and controlled him with their bodies. Women were Samson's kryptonite, stealing his affection and ultimately drawing him away from his covenant with God. Even to the casual observer, Samson appears to be a complete and total idiot in his interactions with Delilah, in that she was very obviously trying to destroy him, not to mention the fact that she was a Philistine. Yet, he behaved as if he were under her spell, yielding his superhuman strength to her devious devices.

LUST AND LOVERS

Unfortunately, bondage to lust is not relegated to just an Old Testament Bible story. The same spirit of lust is at work in many people today. In fact, I had a very close friend who profoundly demonstrated this point. He was wealthy and incredibly intelligent. His journey in his quest for Christ and subsequent fall is an epic story of biblical proportions. He led many people to Jesus in his living room and saw numerous people delivered as the power of the Spirit operated through his hands. Yet my friend had a hidden addiction to porn that led him into a secret life of sex with prostitutes. Consequently, he destroyed his marriage and ruined the lives of his children. Then, just when it seemed like he couldn't get any lower, he was arrested for masturbating in his car in a store parking lot, in broad daylight, with his car door open while calling out to a woman to get her attention. Ultimately, he became a registered sex offender and, years later, he moved in with a prostitute. Unfortunately, my friend became a modern-day Samson. His supernatural strength was siphoned off through porn, prostitutes, and playmates. His covenant with God was annulled, his purity was polluted, and the light in his eyes dulled as the lamp of his soul finally flickered and flamed out.

The sad truth is that my friend's story has become commonplace even among Christians. The number of people addicted to pornography is staggering, and it's growing exponentially every year! Our culture of instant gratification has shackled an entire generation to the monster from the lagoon of perversion and distortion. This has created a massive market for the sex trafficking of women, men, and children—yes, children as young as three years old are being sold to satisfy that monster of molestation, rape, and even murder.

A case in point: Many years ago, I had a friend who dedicated his life to rescuing sex slaves from their traffickers. He was passionate about the mission and created a team of valiant warriors who were fully committed to the cause. Yet the Lord showed me that he was addicted to porn himself. One day, I decided to confront him, and, after a long, hard conversation, he finally confessed! He was blind to the fact that his addiction was actually funding the traffickers he was passionate about extinguishing. He, in fact, had become the victim's customer.

MARRIAGE AS SPIRITUAL WARFARE

Many of us live in a constant state of bondage and blindness simply because we don't know how to manage our passions. Our life can become an ash heap, a monument to our lack of discernment. We need wisdom on how to navigate our urges and fulfill our divine call. It's important to remember that many sins that steal our affection from Christ are *perversions*, meaning that they are the "wrong-version." Often, the antidote for our attraction to the "wrong-version" lies in discovering the "right version." For example, God was the one who gave us a sex drive. When He said, *"Be fruitful and multiply"* (Genesis 1:28), He created human beings with the desire for sex. He designed sex to be intensely pleasurable. I mean, He could have made us like the birds: laying some eggs and taking turns sitting on them until they hatch, having little emotion or passion in the process. Instead, He created orgasms; that's right—it was God's idea!

God even refers to sex in marriage as "spiritual warfare." Check it out for yourself:

> The husband must fulfill his duty to his wife, and likewise also the wife to her husband. The wife does not have authority over her own body, but the husband does; and likewise also the husband does not have authority over his own body, but the wife does. Stop depriving one another, except by agreement for a time, so that you may devote yourselves to prayer, and come together again so that Satan will not tempt you because of your lack of self-control.... But I say to the unmarried and to widows that it is good for them if they remain even as I. But if they do not have self-control, let them marry; for it is better to marry than to burn with passion.
>
> (1 Corinthians 7:3–5, 8–9)

MANY SINS THAT STEAL OUR AFFECTION FROM CHRIST ARE PERVERSIONS, MEANING THAT THEY ARE THE "WRONG-VERSION."

In this passage, the Bible says three things about sex:

1. Married couples have a duty to one another to have sex on a regular basis and not deprive one another. Therefore, the apostle Paul destroyed the myth that Christians should have sex only for the sake of reproduction.

2. When married couples withhold sex from their spouses, they are opening the door to satanic temptation. Thus, healthy sex inside the marriage covenant closes the door to the devil's

devices and undermines his opportunities; so, ultimately, sex is spiritual warfare.

3. One of the reasons for marriage is to give ourselves a healthy outlet to express our sexual desires. Interestingly, *The Message Bible* translates *"burn with passion"* in 1 Corinthians 7:9 as *"sexually tortured"*: *"the difficulties of marriage are preferable by far to a sexually tortured life as a single."*

I am not saying that you should marry just to satisfy your sex drive; the apostle Paul said that. But what I am saying is that managing your sex drive by having sex outside the covenant of marriage is perversion. Furthermore, every perversion has a negative side effect that ultimately costs you exponentially more than its momentary pleasure satisfies you.

In our twenty-first-century society, it has become common to delay marriage for a decade or longer than in previous generations. This isn't necessarily because Christians are trying to be like the apostle Paul and give themselves wholeheartedly to the Lord (though that may be true for some believers). Rather, many people have become perverted, fulfilling their sexual appetites with porn, with the hook-up culture, or by living together with someone in a "friends-with-benefits" relationship. Consequently, the natural sex drive that's in our DNA and helps to motivate us to find our spouse is continually being siphoned off. There is no need to marry anymore because our appetite for sex is being fulfilled through perversion.

THE ALLEY CAT SYNDROME

Humanity has taken on the virtues of an alley cat, which walks the neighborhoods looking for anything in heat. Of course, when you live with no restraints, and your passion is unbridled, it bullies your body into fulfilling its ever-growing demand for an orgasm. So, people behave like heroin addicts whose addiction becomes so consuming that it must feed the fire of its appetite with anything that burns, obtaining these combustibles guided only by its obsession.

Consequently, the aftermath of a virtueless life is a relational destruction derby, whose victims are aborted to avoid the irreversible consequences of living an irresponsible life of pleasure—at the cost of human life. Even birth control isn't enough protection for this instant-gratification generation, which demands pleasure without regard to consequences and must rid themselves of the evidence of their moral violation. Of course, these people mandate that the law of the land allow for this senseless destruction of human life so that the narcissistic, self-absorbed, pleasure-driven society can perpetuate its need to live without restraint and take no responsibility for its actions.

Meanwhile, back in the womb, the silent screams of the innocent cry out for mercy. It's okay: nobody is listening because they are too young to vote!

Our society of perversion mirrors the Philistine culture that Samson was called to destroy some three thousand years ago. The Philistines worshipped Baal, Astarte, Asherah, and Dagon. These false gods (especially Baal and Dagon) required child sacrifices in their worship, in which people would burn their children alive on their altars. Interestingly, Dagon was the god of prosperity. It's disgusting, yet insightful, that the god of prosperity required the sacrifice of children to himself in the days of Samson because much of our society today is sacrificing its children on the same altar. Samson, as I pointed out already, was sent to bring down the perverted Philistine empire, but he was actually infected by the same perversion. His journey to being deceived by Delilah, which ultimately destroyed him, was riddled with sexual exploits along the way.

STAND STRONG IN EVERY SEASON

Ultimately, like Samson, we are commissioned to destroy the works of the enemy and open the door for society to experience the love and power of a superior kingdom. But we can't conquer what we refuse to confront. Jesus put it like this: "*The ruler of the world* [the devil] *is coming, and he has nothing in Me*" (John 14:30). It's imperative that we can honestly say, "The devil has nothing on me because he has nothing in me!" Our spiritual superpower isn't rooted in a Nazirite covenant with God demonstrated by the hair that covers our heads; instead, it's founded on the new covenant in Jesus, whose headship covers the body of Christ and whose power transforms us from sinners into saints! Jesus sent His Spirit to live in us so that His power can metamorphose us from the inside out.

WE ARE COMMISSIONED TO DESTROY
THE WORKS OF THE ENEMY AND
OPEN THE DOOR FOR SOCIETY TO
EXPERIENCE THE LOVE AND POWER
OF A SUPERIOR KINGDOM.

Yet, unlike Samson, who had supernatural strength to destroy sinners, our supernatural authority gives us the power to destroy sin, death, hell, and the grave as we save sinners! (See, for example, Luke 10:19.) For sin can't defeat us, death can't contain us, hell can't have us, and the grave can't hold us! We are royal citizens of a superior kingdom, sent to destroy the ultimate enemy of the Philistines—I mean, we were all once Philistines: enemies of God, held captive by the Delilah of our souls. We were seduced and deceived into believing that freedom meant living an unrestrained life, with unbridled passion, giving way to every temptation and doing it all for the sake of pleasure. Then we met the King of glory, whose kingdom "*is not eating and drinking, but righteousness and peace and joy in the Holy Spirit*" (Romans 14:17). We came to realize that happiness is rooted in happenings, but joy is rooted in Jesus. The events happening around us don't dictate the level of delight we can have within us. Consequently, we are no longer prisoners of our passions, addicted to our appetites and held captive by our shame. I love the way the apostle Paul put it:

> *Therefore if you have been raised up with Christ, keep seeking the things above, where Christ is, seated at the right hand of God. Set your mind on the things above, not on the things that are on earth. For you have died and your life is hidden with Christ in God. When Christ, who is our life, is revealed, then you also will be revealed with Him in glory. Therefore consider the members of your earthly body as dead to immorality, impurity, passion, evil desire, and greed, which amounts to idolatry. For it is because of these things that the wrath of God will come upon the sons of disobedience, and in them you also once walked, when you were living in them. But now you also, put them all aside: anger, wrath, malice, slander, and abusive speech from your mouth. Do not lie to one another, since you laid aside the old self with its evil practices, and have put on the new self who is being renewed to a true knowledge according to the image of the One who created him.* (Colossians 3:1–10)

When we live like this, we become people who stand strong and prosper in every season of life—be it winter, spring, summer, or fall—and through hard times and high times, through abundance or lack, because we know in our "knower" that God works everything out for our good because He loves us! Yet, despite our having these promises and the power of the Holy Spirit within us, plus the wisdom of the age to come upon us, too often, the earth experiences cardboard Christians: shallow believers who live a half-hearted existence. The world is longing for Christians who have enough confidence in their relationship with God that they can say, as Paul did, "Follow me as I follow Christ." (See 1 Corinthians 11:1.) Such believers are those whose holy authenticity and proven character are worth emulating. Their lives hold up under scrutiny, and, the more you know them, the more you respect them.

QUESTION ASKED AND ANSWERED

The "Samson life" of contradiction must die! Power and purity must flow again from the palace. For we are *"a chosen race, a royal priesthood, a holy nation, a people for God's own possession, so that* [we] *may proclaim the excellencies of Him who has called* [us] *out of darkness into His marvelous light"* (1 Peter 2:9). This is *who we are!* Therefore, it's imperative that we answer the question "How then shall we live?"

The world has stopped asking this question because so few people are walking in the high call of God in Christ. We have convinced the world that we are "not perfect, just forgiven." In other words, the difference between non-Christians and Christians is simply forgiveness. This is another perversion—a half-truth that, when separated from the rest of the gospel, is a different gospel altogether! The blood of Jesus didn't just forgive us—it transformed us into new creatures in Christ. (See 2 Corinthians 5:17.) Holiness is not first a requirement; it's a promise! God has given us the power to live a holy life; all we have to do is receive it and walk it out.

THE WORLD IS LONGING FOR CHRISTIANS WHO HAVE ENOUGH CONFIDENCE IN THEIR RELATIONSHIP WITH GOD THAT THEY CAN SAY, AS PAUL DID, "FOLLOW ME AS I FOLLOW CHRIST."

THE SAMSON IN US IS DEAD

The apostle John wrote the clearest exhortation I have ever heard on the life of the believer in relation to sin. Funny—I hardly ever hear this portion of Scripture quoted by leaders or followers of Christ today. I dare you to read it slowly and let it sink deep into your soul! Furthermore, if you are one of those people who call themselves "forgiven but not perfect," please tell me how you can rationalize having a dualistic view of following Christ. Is this not at the root of the Samson culture that is so prevalent in the church today, even among leaders? Okay, here is the exhortation; try reading it out loud:

> *See how great a love the Father has bestowed on us, that we would be called children of God; and such we are. For this reason the world does not know us, because it did not know Him. Beloved, now we are children of God, and it has not appeared as yet what we will be. We know that when He appears, we will be like Him, because we will see Him just as He is. And everyone who has this hope fixed on Him purifies himself, just as He is pure. Everyone who practices sin also practices lawlessness; and sin is lawlessness. You know that He appeared in order to take away sins; and in Him there is no sin. No one who abides in Him sins; no one who sins has seen Him or knows Him. Little children, make sure no one deceives you; the one who practices righteousness is righteous, just as He is righteous; the one who practices sin is of the devil; for the devil has sinned from the beginning. The Son of God appeared for this purpose, to destroy the works of the devil. No one who is born of God practices sin, because His seed abides in him; and he cannot sin, because he is born of God.* (1 John 3:1–9)

Yikkers... *"The one who practices sin is of the devil"*! We are born again, and, therefore, we have received a new nature that includes a new heart and the mind of Christ. (See, for example, Ezekiel 36:26; 1 Corinthians 2:16.) We are no longer sinners but saints. It's not our nature to sin, for we have become the righteousness of God in Christ Jesus. (See 2 Corinthians 5:21.) We once were darkness, but now we are the light of the world. (See Ephesians 5:8.) The Samson in us is dead;

the old man, who was called by God but infected by hell, addicted to sin, and shackled by shame, is *dead*. May he rest in peace!

Here is a direct quote from the Master Himself: "*Therefore you are to be perfect, as your heavenly Father is perfect*" (Matthew 5:48). We are forgiven and perfect in Jesus. Perfection in Him is the goal; anything less than this is a perversion. Again, this is first a promise—Jesus is at work within us, perfecting us—and then it is a command. We can't do this without Him, but we *aren't* without Him! He is at work *in* us, *on* us, and *through* us. So, let's shake off the doctrine of well-meaning but deceived people who lower the standard of life in Christ to soothe their conscience and end up undermining His promise. And let's walk in our high calling as royal, noble sons and daughters of an incredible King!

9

THE ME I HARDLY KNOW

I met Danny Silk in Weaverville, California, when he was sixteen years old. We worked together for about a year at a local tire and repair shop; I managed the repair shop, and he was our tire buster, mounting and fixing tires. Danny was taking drugs and living with his girlfriend at the time. His life was a mess as he hung out with addicts and drug pushers. I shared Jesus with him nearly every day that year, but he was totally disinterested. However, a few years later, Danny came by my service station and asked, "How do you go to church? I mean, they aren't going to just let me walk in there, right?" I smiled and said, "I'll meet you in the parking lot, and we'll go in together." The next Sunday, I met him at the church and welcomed him into the sanctuary. I don't think Danny had ever been to church in his entire life, yet he seemed excited to be there. As the service wrapped up and the crowd began to thin, he turned to me and said, "I want to do the 'thing.'" I motioned to Bill Johnson and said, "Hey, this guy wants to get saved!"

Danny met Jesus that day, and, from that day on, everything began to change in his life. But what happened next dramatically accelerated his spiritual growth. About a month later, a prophet named Dick Joyce came to our church and called Danny out from among the congregation. He gave him a powerful prophetic word about being a world changer. The thing is, no one in our congregation (except for me) knew Danny's past because his friend circle didn't include our people. Consequently, their only knowledge of him was from the prophetic word, so they related to him future-present and not past-present. Our people's faith in Danny accelerated his growth because they were constantly calling him into his prophetic destiny. A few years later, he became Mountain Chapel's senior pastor! Today, Danny is a highly sought-after international conference speaker, the author of several books, the founder of Loving on Purpose (an organization that helps develop whole and healthy families), and a respected senior leader at Bethel Church.

TO BE OR NOT TO BE

Honestly, I don't think I have ever witnessed anyone experience such a fast and intensive spiritual transformation as Danny did in those early years. Furthermore, Danny became a prototype for many others—I literally observed a couple hundred people find Jesus and change their lives from the inside out in our tiny mountain community. I have often pondered those years and asked myself why so many people experienced such a deep and profound transformation at Mountain Chapel. Of course, Jesus is the ultimate, overarching answer to that question. His grace saves, heals, and delivers us from our old life of sin, and transforms us into a whole new creation! Yet, the frequency, speed, and depth of people's conversions in those days was no less than epic much of the time.

There is a common denominator in every single conversion that I have studied at Mountain Chapel, and that common denominator is the prominent prophetic culture that was pervasive throughout the spiritual community there. This all began with prophets and other people with the gift of prophecy who frequented Mountain Chapel on a regular basis. Nearly all of them shared personal prophetic words for our congregation, calling individuals out of the audience and releasing specific messages from God to each of them. Furthermore, those who received prophetic words were instructed to transcribe them and pour over them in prayer, asking for God's wisdom on how to actualize these words. All this led to our being submerged in a culture that knew us through the eyes of the Spirit and related to us according to our high call and not in relation to our pitiful past.

This type of culture was common in the early church. The great apostle Paul laid the foundation for this environment in 2 Corinthians 5:16: *"Therefore from now on we recognize no one according to the flesh; even though we have known Christ according to the flesh, yet now we know Him in this way no longer."* The next verse is one of the most repeated Scriptures from the entire Bible: *"Therefore if anyone is in Christ, he is a new creature; the old things passed away; behold, new things have come"* (verse 17). The connotation is that our old life is gone! Our sins have been forgiven, and we have had a heart transplant; our old man is dead, and we are a whole new person in Christ. In fact, the word *"new"* in this verse has the implication of "prototype," which indicates never before created.[19] Therefore, we recognize one another according to our spiritual rebirth, not our polluted past. But here is the million-dollar question: Do *you* recognize, relate to, and think of yourself according to your new-creation perspective, or—metaphorically speaking—are you stuck in caterpillar mode, having post-traumatic stress disorder from the cocoon experience, and are you afraid of heights so that you refuse to fly? Which reality are you living from?

It's evident that Timothy, Paul's disciple, struggled with his identity in Christ even though he was the senior apostle of the church at

---

19. "G2537–kainos–Strong's Greek Lexicon (KJV)," Blue Letter Bible, accessed July 2, 2025, https://www.blueletterbible.org/lexicon/g2537/kjv/lxx/0-1/; "2537. kainos," NASB Lexicon, Bible Hub, https://biblehub.com/greek/2537.htm.

Ephesus, one of the most famous churches in the entire New Testament. Paul wrote to Tim, his son in the faith, several times, challenging him to live with confidence in his prophetic destiny and purpose. Here's an example of Paul's exhortations:

> *This command I entrust to you, Timothy, my son, in accordance with the prophecies previously made concerning you, that by them you fight the good fight, keeping faith and a good conscience, which some have rejected and suffered shipwreck in regard to their faith.*
>
> (1 Timothy 1:18–19)

DO *YOU* RECOGNIZE, RELATE TO, AND THINK OF YOURSELF ACCORDING TO YOUR NEW-CREATION PERSPECTIVE, OR—METAPHORICALLY SPEAKING—ARE YOU STUCK IN CATERPILLAR MODE?

Notice that Paul's exhortation is for Timothy to live his life according to the prophecies he had received; in other words, to live future-present and not past-present. Later, in the same letter to the apostle Timothy, Paul wrote:

> *Let no one look down on your youthfulness, but rather in speech, conduct, love, faith and purity, show yourself an example of those who believe. Until I come, give attention to the public reading of Scripture, to exhortation and teaching. Do not neglect the spiritual gift within you, which was bestowed on you through prophetic utterance with the laying on of hands by the presbytery. Take pains with these things; be absorbed in them, so that your progress will be evident to all. Pay close attention to yourself and to your teaching;*

persevere in these things, for as you do this you will ensure salvation both for yourself and for those who hear you. (1 Timothy 4:12–16)

Here, Paul gave Timothy another strong exhortation to give himself completely to the spiritual gift that had been imparted to him by the presbytery. In the first-century church, the presbytery was made up of respected spiritual elders; these often included apostles and prophets, leaders who gave oversight to several local churches. By nature of their calling to equip the saints, and by the authority vested in them in Christ, they carried spiritual gifts that they were commissioned to impart to the body of Christ to establish believers in ministry.

CHANGED INTO ANOTHER MAN

One of the best examples of the way in which a prophetic culture affects our personal identity and our life's calling is the story of Saul in the Old Testament. Saul was a farm boy who set out to find his father's lost donkeys. While in pursuit, Saul encountered the prophet Samuel, who had already been briefed by God about Saul's donkey-search situation. Samuel stunned Saul by telling him not only that the donkeys he was searching for had already been found, but also that Saul was highly favored: *"For you shall eat with me today; and in the morning I will let you go, and will tell you all that is on your mind. …For whom is all that is desirable in Israel? Is it not for you and for all your father's household?"* Saul replied, *"Am I not a Benjamite, of the smallest of the tribes of Israel, and my family the least of all the families of the tribe of Benjamin? Why then do you speak to me in this way?"* (See 1 Samuel 9:1–21.)

This encounter is profoundly insightful; Samuel told Saul that, in the morning, he was going to tell him all that was on Saul's mind (better translated as "heart"), which, consequently, turned out to be the fact that Saul was called to be the king of Israel. But here is the kicker: even though Samuel said that kingship was "on Saul's heart," Saul seemed like he had *no idea* he was supposed to be the king! In fact, when Samuel explained to him that he was the desire of all Israel, he pushed back with three reasons why Samuel's declaration couldn't be true: (1) I'm from the wrong tribe. (2) My tribe is small and powerless. (3) My family is the most insignificant group of people in the most irrelevant clan in Israel.

The next morning, the prophet Samuel commissioned Saul to be the king of Israel. (See 1 Samuel 10:1.) The question is, are you spending your life chasing donkeys when you are supposed to be a king or a queen? Has your God-given identity become so lost in the presence of powerless, double-minded people or in decades of poverty or disillusionment that your heart can't even recall your divine purpose? I call this condition "heart dementia," which is the inability to remember your God-given name, your heavenly family, or your high call in Christ Jesus! The symptoms of heart dementia are low self-worth, a lack of confidence, the tendency to hang around disgruntled and unhappy people, and loneliness. It plays out in building cases against people you admire, having a fear of failure, and falling into a victim mentality.

Maybe, as you read this chapter, you are feeling convicted by the Holy Spirit that you have lost sight of your God-given identity, and you wonder how to bust out of the chains of your derailed destiny. Well, the instructions Samuel gave to Saul after making his prophetic declaration over him will be incredibly insightful for you, as well:

> You will come to the hill of God where the Philistine garrison is; and it shall be as soon as you have come there to the city, that you will meet a group of prophets coming down from the high place with harp, tambourine, flute, and a lyre before them, and they will be prophesying. Then the Spirit of the Lord will come upon you mightily, and you shall prophesy with them and be changed into another man.
>
> (1 Samuel 10:5–6)

See what happened when Saul arrived at the hill of God:

> Behold, a group of prophets met him; and the Spirit of God came upon him mightily, so that he prophesied among them. It came

*about, when all who knew him previously saw that he prophesied
now with the prophets, that the people said to one another, "What
has happened to the son of Kish? Is Saul also among the prophets?"
A man there said, "Now, who is their father?" Therefore, it became
a proverb: "Is Saul also among the prophets?"*

(1 Samuel 10:10–12)

Did you notice that Samuel gave the right word to the wrong man?
"Kris, what are you talking about?" you may probe. I mean that Saul
had to be changed into another man to fulfill his prophetic destiny!
Maybe a more accurate explanation is that he had to be changed *back*
into the man he was born to be. The victim mentality ("I was born into
the wrong family"; "I am powerless"; having a small-minded soul, and
so on) hacked the heart of a king and stole his identity. Consequently,
Samuel gave Saul an accurate prophetic word, but it took a prophetic
community, proliferating a prophetic culture, to generate the spiritual
fusion necessary to transform Saul from a pauper into a prince so that
he could fulfill his royal purpose.

The Israelites were so shocked by Saul's sudden conversion that they
began asking one another, *"Is Saul also among the prophets?"*

STAYING CONNECTED

As we read in the rest of 1 Samuel, Saul became the king of Israel
and began his kingship by delivering the Israelites from their notorious
archenemy, the Philistines. But his greatness was short-lived because
he refused to stay connected to the prophetic community that had cat-
alyzed his divine personhood. Consequently, he reverted to his inse-
cure, jealous, pauper mentality and ultimately became a schizophrenic
madman.

Of course, Saul is an extreme case; there are not very many of us
who experience such a dramatic shift in our personhood by being in the
presence of a prophetic community—or being estranged from one. Yet

his life stands out as a profound example of the effect that a group of prophetic people, living in community, can have on one another's lives. As I pointed out earlier, I have personally observed power being released in a small, seemingly insignificant church that became a tight-knit community of prophetic people who transformed the lives of hundreds of broken souls—because I was one of them!

BAR 717

My spiritual journey is well-known to many people because I have shared it so many times, including in portions of this book, but there is a profound yet private part of my journey that I rarely talk about. As I related in chapter 5, when I was barely making it after my first nervous breakdown, Kathy and I moved from San Jose, California, a city of about a million people, to Lewiston, California, a town of nine hundred people nestled in the Trinity Alps. Lewiston is about as far away from society as you can get without completely falling off the earth. We moved there because I was struggling with feelings of hopelessness and was desperate to find peace. I was growing more suicidal by the day, and with a young wife and newborn baby, I was frantically looking for deliverance from this nightmare.

I mentioned earlier that, when I first attended Mountain Chapel, I would sit in the back of the church, and I would need to get up several times during the service to go outside because I had panic attacks and extreme social anxiety. By the time the service was over, I would be soaked in sweat to my underwear. When Bill and Beni Johnson became our pastors, Kathy's and my life was completely transformed. Bill had a holy obsession with the supernatural, especially with healing and prophetic ministry. During his first year there, Bill decided we should have a men's retreat at a lodge so remote that they called it "Bar 717." The lodge was a three-hour drive from Weaverville—in the middle of nowhere. I felt there was no way I was going to go, because I had severe claustrophobia and couldn't ride in a car for that long without puking from anxiety.

But, somehow, the guys from the church talked me into going, with the help of my very persuasive wife, Kathy. I rode in a Jeep with five other guys on the way there, crawling out of my skin with fear. During the drive, the guys started talking about the guest speaker; this man had a reputation as a prophet who would call people out of the congregation and tell them what God was saying to them. *I freaked out!* I wanted to jump out of the Jeep. Remember that my panic attacks were rooted in terrible thoughts and images about doing hideous things to people. I knew that the prophet would uncover me as a Christian imposter, and I would be rejected as a wolf in sheep's clothing! But it was too late to turn around. By the time we arrived at Bar 717, I was in a full-on panic attack. It was all I could do to stumble into the lodge. I was trying desperately to hold it together and not have a complete mental breakdown.

When the meeting finally started, I sat in the back and prayed my guts out that the prophet wouldn't see me. The worship was long and intense as forty guys sang with passion. Then the prophet made his way to the podium, singing in tongues while waving his hands wildly in the air. He looked like a prophet: sort of scary, holy, and powerful, all at the same time—and, most of all, definitely not of this world. My heart was pounding so hard that I could hear it beating like a drum in my ears. The prophet taught for a little while, and then it happened: without warning, he started pointing to people in the audience and inviting them to come to the front. One of my good friends was first—and then the prophet looked right at me and said, in a deep voice, "Young man, come to the front; the Lord has a word for you!" I was shaking so badly that I barely had enough strength in my legs to get up out of my chair. I slowly trudged to the front like a doomed man going to his execution.

Immediately, the prophet raised his voice in tongues as if a hurricane was somehow blowing inside him. He shouted:

I see you in a terrible storm; the winds of adversity have been
blowing against you, trying to destroy you. But God has found
you faithful, and you are a strong man in the Lord. The Lord is

raising you up as a pillar in the church of Jesus Christ. You and your wife shall be a mother and a father in the Israel of God, which is the church. I decree that you shall be a great teacher, and you shall equip My people. Your children shall be finely fashioned, pillars in my house, says the Lord. You shall take them with you...you shall carry them with you...for you will not outgrow your family, but you will grow them with you. They are your first ministry, and as you grow, they will grow alongside you, and your family shall be great in the kingdom!

The prophetic word went on for several more minutes as I wept uncontrollably under the power of God. Thankfully, someone had had the presence of mind to record the proclamation on a cassette tape. That night, everything changed for me—everything! I suddenly realized that God loved me and, just as important, was proud of me. I wasn't going to go crazy and do something stupid, but I was going to be a minister—a man of God—and my family was going to prosper!

The guys were so excited for me. It was as if I were at the finish line at the Boston Marathon, and I was in first place. Everyone was congratulating me and adding their *amen* to the prophet's word. When I went to my cabin that night, I played that prophetic word over and over on a tape recorder. I just kept rewinding it and playing it again and again. When I finally got home after the retreat, I walked into my house a different man. I couldn't wait to play the word for Kathy. We sat on the couch and wept together as we listened to it repeatedly. The next day, Kathy transcribed the prophetic word, writing it on a piece of paper. I folded that paper up and carried it with me for the next three years. Every time I started to have a panic attack, I would go into the restroom, pull out my prophetic word, and read it over myself out loud: "The Lord is raising you up as a pillar in the church of Jesus Christ."

When God entered the garden of Eden after Adam ate the fruit from the forbidden tree, He called out, "Adam, '*Where are you?*'" (Genesis 3:9). I guess if God can't find you, you are really lost! Yet, the truth is, I don't think God was asking Adam for his geographic location; I think He was asking Adam where his heart was positioned, where he stood in his relationship with his Creator. In my own life, and in my relationship with others, I have discovered that prophetic ministry reminds us of our divine purpose, unlocks God's perspective of us, and draws us into His loving arms. I hear the Lord saying, *"Adam, come near! Return to your former glory, to the beauty and innocence of the garden—to the paradise of walking in the cool of the day with Me!"* Do you hear the Lord calling you?

PROPHETIC MINISTRY REMINDS US OF OUR DIVINE PURPOSE, UNLOCKS GOD'S PERSPECTIVE OF US, AND DRAWS US INTO HIS LOVING ARMS.

IT'S A FAMILY AFFAIR

The truth is that our identity, destiny, and purpose are discovered only in relationship with God and our faith community. The Bar 717 experience changed my life not only because I carried the prophetic word with me for three years so that it could be instilled in my heart and life, but also because the men who were in the lodge that night heard what God thought of me and became my strongest encouragers. When I felt down, they reminded me that I was a man destined for greatness. Furthermore, they postured themselves to be taught by me and valued my input in their lives. My leaders, who were in the room that night, acknowledged the favor on my life and promoted me. In fact, if it hadn't been for Bill Johnson, Kathy and I never would have stepped into our divine destiny. In other words, nobody ever succeeds alone! A prophetic word can direct our lives, but it takes a prophetic culture, infused in a prophetic community, to change us into the people we need to be to fulfill our divine purpose.

If you are struggling to find your identity, consider joining a prophetic community. There are many great churches around the world that have cultivated a healthy prophetic culture. If you happen to live in a prophetic "desert" without such a church, there are some great online prophetic communities that you can become a part of in order to learn, grow, and gain a sense of destiny and belonging.[20] It's time to step into your high calling and fulfill God's plan for you!

---

20. Bethel Church has a prophetic online community called "Emerging Prophets" where you can build relationships with other people who are passionate about being part of a prophetic family. To find out more about Emerging Prophets, go to http://epmasterclass.com.

10

PROPHECIES WITH EXPIRATION DATES

My life has been guided by supernatural occurrences, prophetic words, and dreams and visions since I was a teenager. In fact, my salvation was inspired by an encounter with God. It began when I was fifteen years old. My mother was sick with psoriasis that covered most of her body. To make matters worse, for nearly a year, a prowler had been trying to break into our home, prompting us both to sleep with a gun by our side at night. The police were also staking out our house nearly every night to try to catch this perpetrator. The guy actually got into my bedroom one night—I woke up just in time to see him coming through my window. Half asleep, I shouted at him as he leaped out the window. These were trying times for my family, and, as the oldest of three children without a father in the home, I felt like the weight of the world was on my shoulders.

In the midst of all this chaos, one day, lying in my bed in the wee hours of the morning, I said out loud, "If there is a God, if You heal my mother, I will find out who You are and serve You for the rest of my life!" A moment later, an audible voice said, "My name is Jesus Christ, and you have what you requested!" The next morning, my mother was completely well of the psoriasis; and, within a few days, the police apprehended the prowler. Needless to say, our life became substantially more peaceful. After about a week had passed, the voice returned again in the middle of the night, saying, "My name is Jesus Christ. You said that if I healed your mother, you would serve Me, and I am waiting!"

For three long years, I searched for the God who had spoken to me, going from church to church on Sunday mornings. Finally, when I was eighteen, my desperate journey came to an end in a house filled with hippies. That night, I gave my heart to Jesus and kept my promise to follow Jesus for the rest of my life. It would be years before I realized that I was part of the "Jesus People" movement.

"HISTORY WILL TELL US IF YOU BELIEVE ME!"

Fast forward a decade—a year after I was restored from my first nervous breakdown that had begun in my bathtub. I had another bathtub experience—this time a positive one—in addition to the one in which I received the revelation about our being either a thermometer or a thermostat of our environment. (I guess the bathtub has become my prayer closet.) But this particular encounter would forever transform my life! I was lying in the tub reading my Bible when I heard a strange noise. I looked up in time to see Jesus walk through the wall and stand in front of me! I sat up in the tub with a sense of awe surging through my being like electricity. I looked up into His face, and I could see the world in His eyes. Then, to my surprise, He began to talk to me: "I have called you to be a prophet to the nations. You will speak before kings and queens. You'll influence prime ministers and presidents. I will open doors for you to talk to mayors, governors, and ambassadors, and to government officials all around the world. You will be a father to many nations, and you will guide many nations into the kingdom. I will put My words in your mouth, and the nations will know that there is a God in heaven who loves them, leads them, and guides the affairs of men!"

The vision lasted for about half an hour as Jesus told me many other things that would happen in my life. I sat there speechless—my mind was swirling with thoughts, while my heart trembled with a sort of awesome fear, excitement, and wonder. The Lord turned to leave the room. Then He suddenly stopped, turned back around, and pointed right at me, saying in a serious tone of voice, *"History will tell us if you believe Me!"* A moment later, He was gone.

THE PROPHETIC PROCESS CAN TAKE YEARS BEFORE WE REALIZE THE FULFILLMENT OF A DIVINE PROMISE.

Two decades passed before I ever met a politician, and it was a few more years before I had any significant ministry to governmental leaders. These days, I spend a lot of time ministering in that arena. I have learned a lot from that experience. For example, God often calls us to places we are unqualified for and/or uninterested in, which was certainly my situation. Furthermore, I learned to be patient, realizing that the prophetic process can take years before we realize the fulfillment of a divine promise. And, finally, prophecy is often activated by our faith, demonstrated through our actions, attributes, and attitudes; thus, it was necessary for me to believe God by pursuing those in government who were looking for prophetic counsel and not just sit around and wait for them to come to me.

EXPIRATION DATES

Earlier in the book, I described the vision I had of a rocket ship going to the moon. As I watched videos of the Apollo 11 launch and observed the boosters disengaging and falling away, having exhausted all their fuel, I had the profound revelation that we, too, must let go of the encumbrances of our life that once empowered us but have since lost their purpose. Yet one of the greatest challenges we face when the boosters of our life run out of fuel and become encumbrances that need to be released is the effect that this act of release has on our *prophetic* destiny when our purpose is still unfulfilled, delayed, or derailed. The prophet Elijah experienced this dynamic in his personal life. Check out his story with me.

King Ahab and Queen Jezebel led Israel away from Jehovah and into Baal worship, climaxing in the sacrifice of children on altars of worship. The prophet Elijah finally became fed up with their wicked leadership and made a prophetic declaration that it would not rain in Israel for three years. Immediately, rain ceased to fall on the land, forcing Israel to experience a severe famine. Then the Lord spoke to Elijah, saying to him, "*Go away from here and turn eastward, and hide yourself by the brook Cherith, which is east of the Jordan. It shall be that you will drink of the brook, and I have commanded the ravens to provide for you there*" (1 Kings 17:2–4). However, the famine was so harsh that, after a while, the brook dried up, and, apparently, the ravens also stopped coming to feed Elijah. Instead of dying of starvation at the brook in the name of "faithfulness to God's prophetic declaration," or living a life of disillusionment and disappointment because "the promises of God have failed me," Elijah somehow understood that God's prophetic declaration of this provision for him had an "expiration date." Thus, he seems to have pressed into God for further instructions and a new "now word." The Lord then said, "*Arise, go to Zarephath, which belongs to Sidon, and stay there; behold, I have commanded a widow there to provide for you*" (1 Kings

17:8–9). Thankfully, Elijah didn't essentially curse God and die at the brook, like so many of us in the body of Christ do today.

But, wait—the story gets crazier. When Elijah arrived at the widow's house, he discovered that she was stone broke and had no way to provide for him. In fact, she and her son were planning for their own demise: they were going to eat their last meal and die. Yet Elijah refused to be disillusioned or disappointed by the Lord's promise of provision through the widow. Instead, he realized that God's provision wasn't in the widow but in the word! Consequently, he stepped into his prophetic mantle and prophesied God's provision into their lives! Ultimately, God sustained Elijah, the widow, and her son supernaturally for the remaining years of the famine by causing their flour and oil to continuously multiply. (Read the full story in 1 Kings 17:8–15.)

WHEN TO HOLD THEM, AND WHEN TO FOLD THEM

By now, you probably have figured out where I am going with this story. Learning how to relate to prophetic words with wisdom and discernment is absolutely essential to a healthy life in the Spirit. Metaphorically speaking, I have observed many people over the years who refused to leave the brook of prophetic declarations, and therefore they died waiting for the water and the ravens to return to Cherith. They failed to realize that the word was fluid and had an expiration date. They didn't press in for a new "now word" because they were disappointed or even angered by the perceived failed outcome of the first declaration. Jesus clearly taught us, *"It is written, 'Man shall not live on bread alone, but on every word that proceeds out of the mouth of God'"* (Matthew 4:4). Notice that Jesus didn't say, *"…that precedes"*; He said, *"…that proceeds"*! In other words, it's not what God *said* (past tense), but what God *is saying* (present progressive tense), that is the bread of life to our souls.

Here's another example: think about the famous story in which God demanded that Abraham take his son Isaac to the top of a mountain in Moriah and sacrifice him to Jehovah. When Abraham got to the top of the mountain and was ready to make the ultimate sacrifice, he received a new "now word" from God: "Don't sacrifice Isaac." If Abraham hadn't stayed current with God, Isaac would have been killed! (See Genesis 22:1–14.)

Returning to the story of Elijah, imagine what would have happened if Elijah had delayed his response to God and waited too long to go to the brook. Let's suppose for a minute that he had waited until six months into the famine before obeying the Lord's instructions. He would have arrived at a dry creek bed and a birdless aftermath of tragic, delayed compliance.

LEARNING HOW TO RELATE TO PROPHETIC WORDS WITH WISDOM AND DISCERNMENT IS ABSOLUTELY ESSENTIAL TO A HEALTHY LIFE IN THE SPIRIT.

Elijah's story might have ended quite differently if he hadn't obeyed God! Yet disobedience and delayed responses are commonplace in twenty-first-century Christianity. This condition is partly rooted in an overemphasis on grace, which leads us to take no personal responsibility for the fulfillment of the prophetic proclamations that God has assigned to us.

WHEN CIRCUMSTANCES SEEM TO NULLIFY A WORD

It's paramount that we be sensitive to the Spirit's leading, especially when we face circumstances that seem to nullify our prophetic words. For example, in 1996, Kathy and I began to receive several prophetic words about leaving our businesses and joining Bill Johnson's team at Bethel Church in Redding. That same year, Bill invited us to join the

Bethel team, and we were very excited to see what God was going to do. So, in 1998, we sold our three auto-parts businesses for a couple of million dollars to our auto-parts supplier, Big A. Big A was the second largest aftermarket supplier of auto parts in America. We waited for our eighteen-month escrow to close, but then, suddenly, without notice, Big A went bankrupt—the week before they were scheduled to pay us. Their bankruptcy left us $1.8 million in debt and with no auto-parts supplier. When the dust settled and the smoke cleared, we had lost *everything* we had worked for over the course of twenty years. I mean, we lost the house we had built (which was the home where all our kids had grown up) and all of our businesses; we lost everything except for our furniture and our two cars.

To make matters worse, when we first arrived at Bethel (the month before Big A went broke), the church was also going through a financial crisis, of which we were unaware. We knew things were "a little tight," but we had no idea that this meant the staff members were holding their paychecks because Bethel didn't have enough money to cover its payroll. Furthermore, Kathy and I had agreed to work as volunteers for a year until the Bethel School of Supernatural Ministry was up and running. Of course, our strategy had been to live off the profit of our business sale to Big A. Now we were in deep trouble! We had no money, no home, and no paycheck, and we owed 127 suppliers more than $1.8 million! We were desperate!

"WOULD YOU TRUST MY FAITH?"

We met with Bill Johnson and the Bethel Church board to inform the elders that we were quitting Bethel, filing for bankruptcy, and going back to work in the business world so we could recover. I explained all the tearful details to the elders and outlined our exit plan. Abruptly, one of the board members stood up and said, "We don't want you to leave. We are a family, and families stick together in hard times. Furthermore, we are going to pray that Jesus does a miracle in your lives and provides all the money you need to pay off your debts. Would you please consider not going bankrupt for six months so that we can see a miracle of provision happen in your lives?"

"I have no faith for that," I replied.

"Would you trust my faith for six months?" he challenged.

"Well, what's six months when you owe millions? Sure, we will delay all of our plans for six months while we wait on a miracle," I conceded.

Within a month, we were forgiven nine hundred thousand dollars of our debt! Three years later, we were debt-free and working toward rebuilding our financial lives, all while making a salary of about two thousand dollars a month. Everywhere we went, God prospered us. For instance, we bought a tiny house for a hundred thousand dollars with a hard-money loan at 14 percent interest (because our credit was terrible). We kept the house for two years, fixed it up ourselves, and sold it for two hundred thousand dollars. We did the same thing the next year with another house and reaped another one-hundred-thousand-dollar profit.

In 2003, I wrote my first manual, entitled *Basic Training for the Prophetic Ministry*. The manual sold like hotcakes—more than fifty thousand copies were sold in two short years. In 2005, I wrote my second book, *The Supernatural Ways of Royalty*, which, to my total surprise, immediately became a best-selling Christian book. Meanwhile, as I have written about in previous chapters, the Bethel School of Supernatural Ministry was exploding. What began with thirty-seven students was nearly doubling every year! By year six, we had over six hundred full-time students in the ministry school, and we were still growing. At the same time, Bethel Church (which had shrunk to less than a thousand people when Bill Johnson took over as the senior leader) was now filled with more than three thousand hungry, radical revivalists.

I began getting hundreds of invitations to speak all over the world, which opened up so many more opportunities for us. Kathy and I were able to invest much more money into the kingdom than we had made in all the previous years of our businesses combined. The Lord gave us a beautiful house that was three times larger than the house we had lost several years before. That's a great story, so I'll share the abridged version with you. A friend of ours encouraged us to take a look at a house that was for sale on his street, but Kathy refused to look at it because it was very expensive. So, I asked the Lord what to do. (It was a cold winter's day in February, and it was literally pouring rain.) The Lord responded, "I have given you this house, and as a sign that it's yours, it will not rain on the house. In fact, the sun will shine over it today." Kathy reluctantly got into our truck with me, and we drove to see the house. When we arrived, it was pouring rain over the entire neighborhood, yet not a drop of rain fell on the house we were looking at. In fact, the sun was shining on the roof! A month later, we scraped together enough money to buy the house, although things were really tight.

It's been twenty-six years since Kathy and I left Weaverville to follow God's call. I mentioned some of this earlier, but Bethel Church has now grown to more than ten thousand people. Bethel School of Supernatural Ministry (BSSM) is training over five thousand students a year, in three languages, on every continent of the world. We have become the largest vocational school approved by SVES (Homeland Security) in the history of the United States.

ONE THING LEADS TO ANOTHER

"Okay, Kris," you might say, "great story, but how does all this relate to prophetic words and expiration dates?" I'm glad you asked! When Kathy and I lost our businesses and had nothing to return to, and when we learned that Bethel was in so much financial trouble, we could have felt that the Cherith brook had dried up and that God had failed us by causing us to lose everything. We might have moved away from the clear calling of God if we hadn't listened to the counsel of that elder on the Bethel board who literally *stood up and took a stand* by challenging us to trust that God would work things out because He wanted us there.

We all benefit from having faithful counselors in our lives to help us move toward the fulfillment of the God-callings that we sense and the prophetic words that we receive.

What I am getting at is this: If we had left Bethel, we never would have been a part of starting BSSM. If we hadn't started that ministry, I never would have written my first two books or begun speaking around the world. I could go on and on, but I think you catch the idea, which is that, in the fulfillment of His prophetic words, in the same way that He works in all the perplexities and challenges we face, "*God causes **all things** to work **together** for **good** to those who love God, to those who are called according to His purpose*" (Romans 8:28). Our part is to continually listen closely for His "now words."

OUR PART IS TO CONTINUALLY LISTEN CLOSELY FOR GOD'S "NOW WORDS."

CHARTING YOUR PROGRESS

Kathy and I have learned so much about navigating the voice of the Lord in our lives in the last couple of decades since joining the Bethel team. Bethel Church is a highly prophetic community where predictive declarations are commonplace. Yet the mere frequency of prophetic words in our community requires us to embrace the instructions of the apostle Paul, who said, "*Do not quench the Spirit; do not despise prophetic utterances. But examine everything carefully; hold fast to that which is good*" (1 Thessalonians 5:19–21). There are so many prophetic experiences in a culture like Bethel's that there is a temptation to become complacent and actually despise prophetic utterances and quench the Spirit if we don't live with a great deal of wisdom and perseverance.

As you read this chapter, maybe you are struggling to discern whether to press in by faith and obtain your prophetic promise or let the declaration pass because you have spent so much of your life in disobedience that the word may have expired. Of course, it's hard to offer situational wisdom when I don't know your circumstances, but it should suffice to say that there are a few guiding principles that, although conditional, are deeply rooted in truth.

Here are three guiding principles that might help you to navigate your journey forward:

1. *God will never violate His Word or His nature to fulfill His prophecies.* So, for example, the idea that the end justifies the means is simply demonic reasoning!

   A great example of this is the story of when Jesus encountered Satan in the wilderness. Satan offered Jesus *"all the kingdoms of the world and their glory"* if He would just bow down and worship him. (See Matthew 4:8–9.) In the Old and New Testaments, there are many prophesies about all the kingdoms of the world being given to Jesus. Furthermore, we know that the book of Revelation proclaims that, since Christ has risen from the dead, *"the kingdom of the world has become the kingdom of our Lord and of His Christ; and He will reign forever and ever"* (Revelation 11:15). So, we know that it was—and is—the will of God for Jesus to rule over all the kingdoms of the world. But the devil offered Christ a shortcut around the cross to obtain the promise and fulfill His divine purpose. The only issue is that Jesus would have had to violate the Scriptures to worship Satan and expedite His destiny! Of course, Jesus refused to do this, and He thoroughly rebuked Satan with the truth of God's Word. (See Matthew 4:10.) Yet I can't tell you how many times I've watched people violate the bedrock principles of the Scriptures in an attempt to apprehend their prophetic destiny. It always ends in disaster!

2. *God sometimes uses prophecy to test our heart rather than to determine our destiny.* This happened in the case of Abraham when God instructed him to sacrifice his son Isaac but later provided a substitute sacrifice in the form of a ram. (See Genesis 22:1–19.)

God also tested Moses's heart using prophecy. He told Moses that the people's rebellion had come to a tipping point and that He had decided to destroy them and raise up a new nation, putting Moses in charge of it. But Moses pushed back and reminded God of His own prophetic proclamation that He would take *this particular* people into the land of promise! In one of the most stunning turns of events in the entire Bible, *"the* LORD *changed His mind about the harm which He said He would do to His people"* (Exodus 32:14)! How did a mere man change the mind of almighty God? Well, God prophesied doom and then waited to see if Moses would contend for mercy. When he did, God knew that He had the right person in place to lead the nation. (See Exodus 32:1–14.) So, again, sometimes prophecy tests our hearts rather than determines our destiny.

Maybe you have experienced a prophecy that didn't come to pass because the purpose of that prophecy was to test your character, not to guide your destiny. If this is the case, it's time to let go of the prophecy and move forward in God because the purpose of the word has been fulfilled. Hopefully, like Moses and Abraham, you passed the test. If not, you can bet that the test will come again.

3. *God's mercy is never isolated from His justice and righteousness in the fulfillment of His prophecies.* This principle leads us to another prophetic dynamic that is a little hard to discern but probably occurs more often than anyone realizes. It's the dynamic of sympathy that circumvents mercy and is absent of justice. In fact, the difference between sympathy (defined in this way) and mercy is that sympathy is unsanctified compassion. Sympathy is

the result of disconnecting truth from compassion. Jesus sits on a *"mercy seat"* (Hebrews 9:5), but *"righteousness and justice are the foundation of His throne"* (Psalm 97:2). We can't separate mercy from justice and righteousness!

For example, let's say someone has given themselves over to sin and refuses to even acknowledge that they are sinning. They need mercy in their lives, and mercy means that they don't receive the punishment they deserve. But mercy requires the confession of sin; otherwise, if a person refuses to acknowledge their wrongdoing, why would they even think they need mercy? The power of sin is at work in anyone who chooses wickedness and refuses to repent, whether they know it or not. Such a person, being stuck in a cycle of deception, needs truth in order to break free from sin, which has disguised itself as something harmless or maybe even healthy. (See John 8:32.) Sympathetic people will often rush to the defense of deceived ones who are in the throes of discomfort and growing conviction as they're exposed to increasing levels of truth. Yet, ultimately, consequences result from unrepented sin, and those consequences can be very effective in helping a person come to a place of a humility, teachability, and repentance.

The famous story of the prodigal son who wasted his inheritance on pimps and prostitutes illustrates this point so well. The kid wound up eating pods at the pig palace, far from his father's farm. Although his father loved him and ventured out daily into his field of dreams, praying and hoping for his son's return, he refused to turn the farm into a house of prostitution to lure his boy home. Instead, he prepared for his son's righteous and repentant reentry by saving a special robe, ring, and sandals for him. Then, one day, the father had the privilege of greeting his son in the farm field as he made the painful journey home. (See Luke 15:11–25.)

The point is that sometimes we have a prophetic word for the destiny of a person, yet the circumstances in that person's life are moving them in an unrighteous direction, the opposite of the declaration we gave. In our desire to "fix" the situation, we circumvent the ecosystem of sowing and reaping, undermine the power of conviction, and become overly sympathetic to the painful process of repentance in that person's life. If we would just be patient and wait for the process to come to fruition, then we would have the opportunity to extend mercy to the repentant perpetrator. Furthermore, we would see the foundation of righteousness and justice firmly established in their lives.

AN EXHORTATION TO FOLLOW THE SPIRIT

I want to conclude with an exhortation that I shared with you earlier in this chapter:

Do not quench the Spirit; do not despise prophetic utterances. But examine everything carefully; hold fast to that which is good.
(1 Thessalonians 5:19–21)

Go forth and do likewise!

11

WEARING CAMEL'S HAIR: OUT OF STYLE BUT TOTALLY RELEVANT

John the Baptist was out of style but totally relevant. His clothes were detestable, his diet unpalatable, and his message indigestible—and yet his impact on history is undeniable. He was conceived by a miracle, announced by an angel, anointed by the heavenly King, filled with the Spirit, and hated by the world. God was about to send the Messiah to earth to save the world, but He had to send John first to work on the heart-roads of His people.

It's the nature of God to send someone into our lives to offend our minds so that He can reveal our hearts. If you dress like John did, nobody will invite you to speak in the temple; consequently, John spoke only in the wilderness. John was the son of Zacharias, who was a priest. (See Luke 1:5–25.) Although his mom and dad were righteous, John grew up among the religious elite who loved to appear holy and righteous but were really *"whitewashed tombs...full of dead men's bones"* (to quote Jesus in Matthew 23:27). John wanted no part of fame, wealth, or power. He was a Jesus People hippie two thousand years before there was such a thing. He was a countercultural radical who had a large role in fulfilling the prophet Isaiah's declaration about making the *"crooked places...straight and the rough places smooth"* to *"prepare the way of the* LORD." (See Isaiah 40:3–5 NKJV.) In other words, he was sent by God to confront the corrupt religious and political system of his day and to call the nation to repentance.

John's soul wasn't for sale at any price, so he couldn't be bought, and he wasn't afraid of death; therefore, he was an unstoppable force of Holy Spirit power! When the Pharisees showed up to his baptisms, he would shout, *"You brood of vipers, who warned you to flee from the wrath to come?"* (Matthew 3:7). Well, at least his gatherings saved money on ushers, who are tasked with helping people feel welcome and comfortable! There was no worship music to create the mood and no choir; there were no comfortable chairs; heck, for that matter, there were no restrooms and there was no Starbucks nearby. Yet the Bible says, *"Jerusalem was going out to him, and all Judea and all the district around the Jordan; and they were being baptized by him in the Jordan River, as they confessed their sins"* (Matthew 3:5–6).

HEADLESS AND STILL HAUNTING

John's impact wasn't limited to the religious crowd or to the common folk; John called the most powerful governmental leaders of his day to repentance! In fact, King Herod, one of the most notoriously wicked kings of the first century, had taken his own brother's wife in marriage. (What a slimeball!) John publicly rebuked him, shouting to him, *"It is not lawful for you to have your brother's wife"* (Mark 6:18). Herod's adulterous wife, Herodias, hated John, and it turns out that she was no victim. She was a seductive and manipulative harlot who had Herod wrapped around her proverbial finger. She demanded John's head on a platter. Herod and Herodias sought to silence the voice of conviction by beheading John. (See Mark 6:17–28.) But conviction for sin grew exponentially in Herod's life, to the point that he attributed the miracles of Christ to John's having risen from the dead and come back to haunt him. (See Mark 6:14–16.)

When it comes to moral issues in people's lives, we must be gracious, and we must be compassionate; but the one thing we can't be, as the life of John the Baptist illustrates so perfectly, is silent! Our silence has resulted in a morally rudderless society that is misinformed, regularly lied to, and led by people who have exchanged feelings for facts. Noble people will always be blamed for the guilt of the guilty and the convicted consciences of the virtueless who try to silence their inner voice of shame by censoring the voice of dignity.

HOLY ATTRACTION

So, the question remains, why did entire cities go out to the wilderness to hear John insult them with his harsh message of repentance? What was the attraction? I mean, what did he do to appeal to such huge crowds? Didn't people know that John's message wouldn't be encouraging, inspiring, or comforting? Furthermore, wouldn't there have to have been a ton of peer pressure for people to wade into the cold Jordan River, confess their sins in the presence of their neighbors and family, and get baptized? Yet the crowds kept *growing*! Why? There was no marketing, click-bait social media attraction, or conference merch to draw them… just John, doing his God-thing without pomp or gimmicks, in the wilderness, eating grasshoppers and wearing camel's hair. (See Matthew 3:4; Mark 1:6.)

The answer is simple (well, sort of simple) yet profound: *holy attraction!* When the Lord calls us, He puts His favor on us, which, again, is a little hard to explain but easy to experience. His favor is kind of like an invisible tractor beam, pulling people into our vortex and causing them to want to believe us and even assist us in God's purposes. While favor is God's holy attraction, seduction is the devil's counterfeit attraction. The apostle John spoke to the root causes of seduction, putting it like this:

> *Do not love the world nor the things in the world. If anyone loves the world, the love of the Father is not in him. For all that is in the world, the lust of the flesh and the lust of the eyes and the boastful pride of life, is not from the Father, but is from the world. The world is passing away....*   (1 John 2:15–17)

The favor of God doesn't appeal to the lust of mankind's lower nature; instead, it tugs on the nobility resident in every human, because we were all created in the image and likeness of our Creator. Favor inspires true greatness in the depth of our being, while conviction reminds us that we are better than our bad behavior, evil choices, and selfish attitudes. Conviction says, "You are way too awesome to be acting like that!"

The incongruity comes when we try to appeal to the lower nature of humanity with the intent of inspiring a holy outcome in the lives of people. Manipulation is manipulation, even if it's for a holy cause! For example, using fear tactics to raise money for a just cause is evil, no matter how noble the ultimate goal is. The same thing goes for seduction, which is actually rooted in the power of lust and exposes us to witchcraft and every kind of demonic influence. Think about the temptation in the garden of Eden: God created Adam and Eve and put them in charge of the entire planet. He said, "Be fruitful and multiply and subdue the earth." (See Genesis 1:28.) God had planted two distinct trees in the garden—the Tree of Life and the Tree of Knowledge of Good and Evil. He gave the couple instructions to eat from any tree in the garden except for the Tree of Knowledge. In fact, the Knowledge Tree came with this warning label: *"In the day that you eat from it you will surely die"* (Genesis 2:17). The serpent lured Eve into desiring the fruit of this tree, convincing her that eating it would make her wise, like God. When Eve and Adam ate the forbidden fruit, they didn't just disobey God—they obeyed the devil! They changed masters, and the entire planet came under the power of Satan. He became the god of this world by the power of seduction and manipulation!

THE FAVOR OF GOD DOESN'T APPEAL TO THE LUST OF MANKIND'S LOWER NATURE; INSTEAD, IT TUGS ON THE NOBILITY RESIDENT IN EVERY HUMAN, BECAUSE WE WERE ALL CREATED IN THE IMAGE AND LIKENESS OF OUR CREATOR.

HYPE, HIPSTERS, AND HATERS

Today, among believers, there is an obsession with being cool, hip, or in vogue so that we can be relevant, appeal to the masses, and open the door for the gospel. Consequently, the topic of morality is whispered only in the safe company of one's closest friends, and purity has become a well-kept secret. Nobility has virtually disappeared from society, being viewed as an old man's musings, irrelevant to the twenty-first century, hipsters, and the PC crowd. In fact, moral restraint is deemed as bondage that shackles society—promoted only by religious bigots and antiquated "dinosaurs" who are disappearing in the ice age of a Sonless society. And so, we who have a noble purpose cower in the corner of culture, living in the shadows of society, desperately hoping we won't awaken the hipster's dissatisfaction and invite unnecessary persecution for ourselves. Meanwhile, our children march slowly into the darkness as we congratulate ourselves on another day without offense.

BE YOURSELF

In the 1995 movie *Braveheart*,[21] there is a scene where the character of William Wallace, his face painted like a warrior, arrives on his huge black horse and rides back and forth in front of the Scottish militia who are gathered for war. William is trying to inspire them to fight for their freedom from the wicked oppression of the English ruler Longshanks. The Scottish combatants are deflated, discouraged, and scared. They are enormously outnumbered and ridiculously outgunned, with virtually little to no chance of defeating the English. But Wallace's valiant speech convinces the men to stay and fight!

After his exhortation, William rides back to his own small but loyal group of radical warriors, his band of brothers, whose faces are also marked by war paint. One of his soldiers, named Stephen, says, "Fine speech! Now what do we do?" William nods to them, then responds, "Just be yourselves!" They go on to defeat the English on the battlefield that day!

I realize it's just a movie, but I can't help seeing the similarities between the battle they fought, which became a tipping point in the war for their freedom, and the battle we face in our day to free the hearts of men. We all have a race to run and a fight to finish in the war we face to free the world from the bondage of a truly wicked reprobate, Satan. Yet, there is so much pressure to conform to the image of the crowd, to be accepted and loved. Moreover, many in the crowd are in the bondage of sin and are bonded with one another in a kind of "misery loves company," dysfunctional clan. The clan's rules are: (1) fit in or get out, and (2) diversity through common agreement. It preaches inclusivity but oppresses free thinkers and detractors. Yet you were called to be an authentic, one-of-a-kind human. There is so much power in being real—in being an original, not a cheap copy of someone else or a dumbed-down version of yourself.

---

21. *Braveheart*, directed by Mel Gibson (Icon Productions and The Ladd Company, 1995).

Case in point: the Israelites were locked down in terror for forty days while a nine-foot, six-inch giant named Goliath taunted them. On each of those forty days, the giant stood up and shouted, "Send someone out to fight me. If he defeats me, we will all serve you; but if I defeat him, you must all serve us!" Young David just happened to show up on the battlefield on the fortieth day to bring his brothers, who were soldiers in King Saul's Israelite army, some lunch. As fate would have it, he arrived just as the giant stood up and unleashed his rant on Saul's army.

David was stunned by the fact that no one stood up to this challenge, even after King Saul had offered a huge reward to the man who killed that loudmouth, trash-talking, arrogant bully. So, David started asking anyone who would listen, *"What will be done for the man who kills this Philistine and takes away the reproach from Israel? For who is this uncircumcised Philistine, that he should taunt the armies of the living God?"* (1 Samuel 17:26). After David had a run-in with his oldest brother, a soldier finally took David to plead his case to the king. (See 1 Samuel 17:1–31.)

> *Saul said to David, "You are not able to go against this Philistine to fight with him; for you are but a youth while he has been a warrior from his youth." But David said to Saul, "Your servant was tending his father's sheep. When a lion or a bear came and took a lamb from the flock, I went out after him and attacked him, and rescued it from his mouth; and when he rose up against me, I seized him by his beard and struck him and killed him. Your servant has killed both the lion and the bear; and this uncircumcised Philistine will be like one of them, since he has taunted the armies of the living God." And David said, "The Lord who delivered me from the paw of the lion and from the paw of the bear, He will deliver me from the hand of this Philistine." And Saul said to David, "Go, and may the Lord be with you." Then Saul clothed David with his garments and put a bronze helmet on his head, and he clothed him with armor. David girded his sword over his armor and tried to walk, for he had not*

tested them. So David said to Saul, "I cannot go with these, for I have not tested them." And David took them off. He took his stick in his hand and chose for himself five smooth stones from the brook, and put them in the shepherd's bag which he had, even in his pouch, and his sling was in his hand; and he approached the Philistine.

(1 Samuel 17:33–40)

This is a great story from so many perspectives, but for our discussion in this chapter, I want to point out that David killed the giant not as a warrior but as a shepherd. David tried on the garments of a warrior, but they didn't fit the season he was in. David never fought with a sling after that battle. His victory over Goliath facilitated his promotion, and from that day on, he fought with a warrior's arsenal. But Saul's armor never did fit David, because Saul was about a foot taller that anyone in Israel. Furthermore, it's doubtful that David could have defeated Goliath in hand-to-hand combat. But David redefined the rules of engagement; consequently, Goliath brought ground weapons to an air war! David forced the giant into a battle he had never prepared for.

WHEN WE UNDERSTAND OUR SEASON AND EMBRACE OUR GOD-GIVEN IDENTITY, WE REDEFINE THE RULES OF ENGAGEMENT.

When we lose ourselves in the peer pressure of the crowd, we face our giants with Saul's armor, with which our enemies have been training and preparing for decades. But when we understand our season and embrace our God-given identity, we redefine the rules of engagement. Our enemy's weapons are ineffective against the power of authenticity, because he has been training for the crowd—including clones, phonies, and fakes. By the time he figures out that he is facing a one-of-a-kind child of the King, it will be too late for him to regroup or retreat. Our victory is imminent!

Let me pull all this together and see if I can help you understand my perspective. John the Baptist was a weird dude! His camel-hair garment never did become conference merch, and his grasshopper diet—well, let's just say, no celebrities ever hacked his cookbook. But John understood who he was and, frankly, who he wasn't. When Jesus asked John to baptize Him, he refused at first because he understood his role and his position in Christ. Yet Jesus required him to act outside of his perceived mandate, demonstrating to us all that even when we become secure in our identity and sure of our calling, He is still the Lord of our lives!

UNIQUE: THE POWER OF ONE

I was raised by a grandfather who loved me but was about as irrelevant to society as a man could get and still not live in a cave on some uninhabited island. He wore coveralls with no underwear. (I mention his lack of underwear because you would pick up on that fact pretty quickly if you met him, as he didn't button up the side of his coveralls, so you could often see his butt.) Furthermore, he had a gum disease; consequently, he'd had all of his teeth pulled, and he wore dentures, which he called his "chompers." I said he "wore" dentures, but, actually, his false teeth didn't fit correctly. They hurt his mouth, so he kept them sticking out of the upper pocket of his coveralls, where people might normally keep a pair of glasses in case they needed them for reading. Then, he would just plop them in his mouth when he was ready to eat a meal. One more thing: my grandfather hated bathing and wore no deodorant! I can still remember my grandmother arguing with him over his terrible body odor and begging him to bathe. Yet my grandfather was my hero, my mentor, and the most important person in my life. I modeled my life after him until I found Christ.

My grandfather owned farms, service stations, and auto-repair shops (that's where he got the nickname "Sparky"), so I knew what I wanted to do in life from the time I was a young boy. When I was twenty-four years old, Kathy and I bought our first Union 76 service station. Later, we added two more repair shops, three auto-parts stores, and an automotive compressor remanufacturing plant. I had been a terrible student in school, partly because I could barely read. In fact, I read at a third-grade level when I graduated from high school, and I couldn't spell to save my life. My grandfather used to tell me that I was "good with my hands." To me, that sort of meant, "The kid is not very smart, but he is hardworking and a gifted mechanic."

I did great in the automotive business; I *was* good with my hands, learned how to run a small business, and was passionate about taking good care of our customers. Then, as I mentioned previously, when I was forty-three, God called Kathy and me to leave all our businesses behind, move from our home in Weaverville, and go to Bethel Church to start the Bethel School of Supernatural Ministry. Talk about "Crocodile Dundee goes to New York"—oh, man! Nothing my grandfather had taught me was even remotely applicable to life as a public person, much less a preacher of the gospel!

When we arrived at Bethel, I felt the Lord tell me three things: be yourself, do your best, and trust Me completely. Well, that advice proved to be slightly harder to follow than I thought. First of all, I was with Bill Johnson, a fifth-generation pastor and, arguably, one of the best preachers of all time. For the first couple of years, after I preached, I would often receive anonymous letters correcting my theology and/or telling me that my humor decimated the sacredness of the pulpit! My communication style was nothing like Bill's, and my automotive parables were, well, let's just say they were not terribly relevant to people who weren't "good with their hands." There was so much pressure for me to be like Bill; I could feel the tension within me as I tried to mimic his style. For example, Bill never uses notes when he preaches; so, I attempted to be spontaneous, but I found myself with nothing to say! I tried being deep, like Bill, who often shares a profound revelation and then pauses for effect; we call it the "power pause." Unfortunately, when I made a point and paused, people thought I had forgotten my next point! Furthermore, I was receiving a lot of negative feedback about my "unholy humor"; so, I tried not being funny, and I became boring.

Behind the scenes, I was a fish out of water, trying to navigate the religious culture of a megachurch with the leadership skills of a street thug or a mafia boss: no cussing, no harsh confrontation, no sarcasm, and especially no unholy conversations allowed. Compared to the guys I worked with back at the auto shops, I was Billy Graham; but, in light of the sacred culture created by a fifth-generation, nonconfrontational holy man, it's fair to say that there was a noticeable contrast between the impact Bill's leadership had on our team and the effect my leadership had on our team.

About my third year at Bethel, I proactively decided to be myself and trust God. I heard this phrase in my spirit that sort of solidified my decision: "It's better to be hated for who you truly are than to be loved for who you really aren't." When I became authentic, I stopped feeling like a poser, and I just worked on being the best version of myself I could be. I didn't reject the people who criticized me, but I stopped listening to their commentary on my ministry and personhood. Being myself felt so good, although the criticism grew quite a bit. Yet something else was simultaneously taking place: favor was growing in my life, and I was slowly attracting a different kind of person who highly valued being raw, real, and radical. In fact, the more honest I became about my life, the more the hearts of our people trusted me. In a short time, our church culture shifted from being a "ready, aim, aim, aim, shoot" culture to a "ready, shoot, aim" environment. (We had been analyzing things until we were paralyzed, and thus we rarely accomplished much.) Yet, in time, our people learned to enjoy taking risks. I began telling funny stories about some of my ministry moments that had gone wrong and some of the sermon mistakes I had made from the podium. I laughed at myself from the platform and made fun of my own glaring weaknesses. Some of the hyper-spiritual people left as we redefined what it meant to be holy, righteous, and godly. I purposely made fun and laughter one of our core values, which became a large part of our culture.

I was finding myself and letting who I am flow freely from my spirit. I'm not John the Baptist, John the Beloved, or Bill Johnson; I am Kris Vallotton, called to Bethel Church by God Himself to be everything He created me to be: fully alive, honest, vulnerable, authentic, and funny! When we allow ourselves to be unique, the way God created us to be, we will be able to fulfill our callings and make an impact on our society, just as John the Baptist and David did.

WEAKNESSES "R" US

Several years ago, a university that uses some of my books in their curriculum offered me an honorary doctorate. I was excited about the possibility of having a degree. So, I started the two-month process of fulfilling the simple requirements necessary to make it possible. About a month into the process, I woke up in the middle of the night and realized that the Lord was waiting to have a word with me.

He asked, *What do you think you are doing with that university paperwork?*

"Well," I responded (still half-asleep), "I'm getting my degree."

You didn't ask Me about getting a degree! the Lord said in frustration.

"Okay, well…is it okay if I get a degree?"

NO! He answered. *If you have a degree, people will think you can do this, and we both know YOU CAN'T! You are an example of what I can do with weakness.*

Frankly, I was brokenhearted over the situation. I had already called my mom and told her that I was about to get an honorary doctorate.

She had cried over the phone and told me how proud she was of me. But I knew the degree was not up for discussion, and I understood that, ultimately, the Lord was right. Yet the situation opened the door to another revelation about my personhood: I realized that night that I was not just an accumulation of my strengths but also of my divinely fashioned weaknesses! What I mean is that we spend a lot of time trying to discover and develop our gifts and strengths, but God wants us to trust Him to accomplish His will through us! For example, at Bethel, for years, we have used a gifts-assessment curriculum with a corresponding test whose main goal is to help us discover our greatest strengths. While assessments like this help us to better understand our gifts and preferences, I am convinced that when we bring our test scores to the Lord to show Him how He can best utilize us, He often says, *Great, that's where I won't be using you because you know too much in that area to depend on Me!*

GOD HAS DESIGNED US WITH DIVINELY PLACED WEAKNESSES IN OUR SOULS SO THAT OUR VICTORIES WILL BELONG TO HIM AND NOT TO US.

Concerning this subject, the apostle Paul wrote:

He [Jesus] has said to me, "My grace is sufficient for you, for power is perfected in weakness." Most gladly, therefore, I will rather boast about my weaknesses, so that the power of Christ may dwell in me. Therefore, I am well content with weaknesses, with insults, with distresses, with persecutions, with difficulties, for Christ's sake; for when I am weak, then I am strong. (2 Corinthians 12:9–10)

Notice that God didn't indicate, "When you are weak, then I am strong!" but rather "When you are weak, then you are strong!" The apostle Paul is a great example of this divine paradox. He was an expert in Jewish law and had trained under one of the most famous professors/rabbis of his day. (See Acts 22:3.) But when He found Jesus, he became a powerful and effective apostle to the Gentiles, whom he initially knew little about!

Being authentic, embracing your identity, and moving in your calling isn't just about finding your strengths; it's also about discovering your weaknesses. God has designed us with divinely placed weaknesses in our souls so that our victories will belong to Him and not to us. Most of us spend an hour a day in front of the mirror trying to cover up our imperfections. Yet the true beauty of your personhood is not found in a makeover but in the raw, real, and radical you, revealed in all of God's glory. Therefore, here is my conclusion: love yourself, be yourself, laugh at yourself, and trust God to do something great with your life!

12

FRIENDLY SNAKES

Moses met God in a burning bush and was commissioned by Him to free the Israelites from four hundred years of slavery. (See Exodus 3:1–4:17.) Moses had actually tried to free the Jews forty years earlier but had failed miserably. Moreover, Moses had grown up in the palace of Pharaoh, and he knew firsthand that Pharaoh was an unrelenting warrior. (See Exodus 2:1–15.) He understood that freeing the people of God from the clutches of this wicked dictator would be no cakewalk! So, Moses resisted God's request to lead the people in a mass exodus, explaining to the Lord that he was both unqualified (he apparently had a speech impediment) and outmatched by Pharaoh's superior arsenal. But God was unimpressed by Moses's Egyptian civic lesson and his lack of self-confidence. He reminded Moses that He had made his mouth. (I guess His point was that if He had made Moses's mouth, then He could certainly fix it.) God went on to demonstrate the fact that Pharaoh's arsenal was no match for the weapons of warfare that would be unleashed on Egypt if Pharaoh decided to resist the will of the Creator of the universe.

Moses was carrying a shepherd's rod because he was a sheepherder. God instructed him to throw down his staff—and suddenly it became a snake. Moses's first response was to run from the snake because men and snakes are natural enemies. But after a public demonstration of this "snake trick" to the children of Israel, and an evidently private commissioning of his older brother Aaron to do the same with his staff, Moses set out with his brother to confront the cunning king of Egypt. (See Exodus 4:27–31.)

Moses and Aaron demanded that Pharaoh release all the Israelite slaves at once, or it was going to get really ugly! But the king blew off their threats and ignored their demands. They immediately initiated the divine plan and invoked the name of God in their ultimatum to free the slaves. Yet, again, the powerful, arrogant, narcissistic ruler brushed off their threats and taunted the God of Moses. On cue, Aaron threw down his staff, and it became a snake. But Pharaoh invoked the sorcerers to challenge God's snake. The sorcerers all threw down their staffs, and a den of vipers emerged, demonstrating the power of witchcraft! But Aaron's God-snake devoured all of the sorcerers' serpents in seconds. (See Exodus 7:8–13.)

Thousands of years later, as we recount the Israelite exodus from Egypt, we are struck by the fact that it was God's snake that would initiate a revolution in Pharaoh's court, ultimately leading to the freeing of God's people. Yet there is a deeper lesson here, being played out in the sands of the Egyptian desert: the enemy saw the persuasive power of Aaron's snake and, consequently, had his sorcerers duplicate the miracle of God. God went on to increase the severity of His demand for the freedom of His people by invoking ten plagues against the Egyptian pharaoh. But the sorcerers were able to mirror the first two of Moses's miracles—turning water to blood and reproducing the frog plague! Consequently, Pharaoh was unmoved by the plagues of God, and he relentlessly taunted Moses and Aaron. But the pharaoh of Egypt had no idea who he was messing with, because the God of the universe had demanded a favorable response from this puny, pitiful earthling, and He had no intention of taking no for an answer. By the time God finished shaking down the rebellious evil dictator, Egypt was in shambles, Pharaoh's son lay dead, and the economy of the country was completely destroyed.

Pharaoh couldn't rid himself of the Israelites fast enough and finally let the people go. Yet the bipolar nature of hatred seethed in his heart. In a rage, he set out with his powerful army to annihilate the people of God. Pursuing them and trapping them at the Red Sea, he thought that he would finally enact his revenge against the God of heaven. Just when things looked really bleak for the Israelites, Moses raised his snake staff, and suddenly the sea parted. With no time to spare, the people rushed across the dry seabed, with Pharaoh in hot pursuit. But the God of the universe had one more trick up His proverbial sleeve: Moses raised his snake staff one last time, and the Red Sea closed its corridor, drowning the entire Egyptian army in the ocean of their rebellion. (See Exodus 7:14–12:50; 13:17–14:31.)

Today, millions of people live in the clutches of an evil "pharaoh," enslaved by Satan's demonic powers and controlled by fear and manipulation. Yet, once again, God has initiated a plan to destroy the works of darkness and free the earth from the bondage of this wicked prince. And, once again, He has commissioned His deliverers and empowered them with supernatural gifts to demonstrate the might of a much superior kingdom. In fact, the eleven disciples had a burning-bush encounter with God after Jesus's resurrection when they experienced the outpouring of the Spirit at Pentecost. Earlier, Jesus had told them, *"Behold, I am sending forth the promise of My Father upon you; but you are to stay in the city until you are clothed with power from on high"* (Luke 24:49). The Lord's instructions were specific and concise: don't leave Jerusalem until you are clothed with power! The apostle Paul reinforced the need for supernatural demonstrations when he wrote, *"For the kingdom of God does not consist in words but in power"* (1 Corinthians 4:20).

COUNTERFEIT PHILOSOPHIES

It was a snake that initiated a revolution in Pharaoh's court, ultimately leading to the freeing of God's people. The enemy saw the power of the snake and, consequently, had his sorcerers duplicate the miracles of God. Today, the devil has devised the same devious plan, counterfeiting the miracles of God to convince many believers that all supernatural power is witchcraft and, therefore, that all demonstrations of power are evil! Think about this brilliant plot. Jesus said, "Don't leave the city until you are clothed with power." The devil knows he is no match for the power of God, so he must figure out a way to convince us to keep our weapons holstered while he robs our house, kills our children, and destroys our family.

When we imagine demonic warfare, we often think of getting a flat tire on the way to church, sickness that persists in our lives, or the immorality that's growing in society. Symptoms like these can be—and often are—manifestations of spiritual warfare; but I am not convinced that they are at the epicenter of the most evil devices of Satan's strategy. The Bible says that Satan *"disguises himself as an angel of light"* (2 Corinthians 11:14). In other words, the devil's work can look good or maybe even healthy. Does causing a flat tire seem good? No. Or does convincing someone to commit sexual immorality seem like a stealth move, appearing to be light or of noble purpose? No! So, what types of things demonstrate "angel-of-light" kind of warfare or "wolves in sheep clothing" deception? Let's examine Jesus's warnings about false prophets and see if we can expose the most diabolical, devious, and destructive strategy ever unleased against humans. Here are the Lord's warnings in His own words:

> If anyone says to you, *"Behold, here is the Christ,"* or *"There He is,"*
> do not believe him. For false Christs and false prophets will arise

and will show great signs and wonders, so as to mislead, if possible,
even the elect. (Matthew 24:23–24)

Beware of the false prophets, who come to you in sheep's clothing, but
inwardly are ravenous wolves. You will know them by their fruits.
Grapes are not gathered from thorn bushes nor figs from thistles, are
they? So, every good tree bears good fruit, but the bad tree bears bad
fruit. A good tree cannot produce bad fruit, nor can a bad tree pro-
duce good fruit. Every tree that does not bear good fruit is cut down
and thrown into the fire. So then, you will know them by their fruits.
Not everyone who says to Me, "Lord, Lord," will enter the kingdom
of heaven, but he who does the will of My Father who is in heaven will
enter. Many will say to Me on that day, "Lord, Lord, did we not proph-
esy in Your name, and in Your name cast out demons, and in Your
name perform many miracles?" And then I will declare to them, "I
never knew you; depart from Me, you who practice lawlessness."
(Matthew 7:15–23)

Here are six powerful points Jesus makes about false prophets:

1. There will be false prophets in our midst.

2. These false prophets will have real power.

3. The miracles they display will be exactly the same kinds of supernatural acts that Christians are supposed to walk in to demonstrate the power of a superior kingdom.

4. The goal of their ministry will be to lead people astray.

5. It will be hard to tell the real from the false, because even *"the elect"* must beware.

6. A fruit check will unearth the false prophets' rotten root system.

Okay, let's dig into this a little deeper. Jesus commissioned us, saying:

Go into all the world and preach the gospel to all creation. He who has believed and has been baptized shall be saved; but he who has disbelieved shall be condemned. These signs will accompany those who have believed: in My name they will cast out demons, they will speak with new tongues; they will pick up serpents, and if they drink any deadly poison, it will not hurt them; they will lay hands on the sick, and they will recover. (Mark 16:15–18)

Notice that supernatural acts are supposed to follow *everyone* who believes! Now let's review the aftereffects of the first Holy Spirit outpouring after Jesus rose from the dead and told His disciples to wait to be *"clothed with power from on high"* (Luke 24:49):

Peter, taking his stand with the eleven, raised his voice and declared to them: "Men of Judea and all you who live in Jerusalem, let this be known to you and give heed to my words. For these men are not drunk, as you suppose, for it is only the third hour of the day; but this is what was spoken of through the prophet Joel: 'And it shall be in the last days,' God says, 'That I will pour forth of My Spirt on all mankind; and your sons and your daughters shall prophesy, and your young men shall see visions, and your old men shall dream dreams; even on My bondslaves, both men and women, I will in those days pour forth of My Spirit and they shall prophesy.'" (Acts 2:14–18)

The first Holy Spirit outpouring manifested in believers speaking in tongues, prophesying, and having spiritual dreams and visions. Yet the false prophets claim the same power: "Didn't we prophesy, cast out demons, and perform many miracles in your name?" You may ask, "Kris, where are you going with this?" Well, just as the devil couldn't stop Moses and Aaron, he can't stop us from demonstrating the power of God, so he duplicates it. Think about it: the greatest consequence of the sorcerers' mirroring the miracles of God is that those authentic demonstrations of supernatural power that were supposed to prove that God had indeed sent Moses to deliver His people were undermined.

When the sorcerers were able to perform the same miracles, the power of persuasion was nullified. So, what was the divine solution? To stop doing miracles because it was causing too much confusion? *No!* God just kept increasing the levels of demonstration until even the sorcerers admitted, "This must be from God, because we can't perform these miracles!" (See Exodus 8:19.) Can you imagine what would have been the outcome if Moses had become discouraged by Pharaoh's taunting and stopped doing miracles, while the sorcerers continued to move in demonic power?

THE WAR OF THE WORLDS

The truth is that we are engaged in the war of the worlds, yet this war is not being fought over territories, countries, or wealth but over the hearts of men! This is why Paul warned us, *"Take up the full armor of God, so that you will be able to resist in the evil day, and having done everything, to stand firm. Stand firm therefore…"* (Ephesians 6:13–14). Yet one of the greatest challenges of our day is that the global church has largely had the opposite response to Satan that Moses had in his confrontation with the king of Egypt. Again, when we see people in the New Age movement, satanists, cultists, and those who practice the occult demonstrating supernatural power, many of us run from true demonstrations of God. We fear (rightfully so) that we will be considered guilty of participating in something evil—either by association or by actually working for the dark side!

However, the consequence of our reacting to the crowd of accusation is that we are quickly becoming a powerless, "non-prophet" organization, while we confront an enraged demonic lunatic who will stop at nothing to destroy humanity. The church has, for the most part, abandoned its mandate to destroy the works of the devil; in its place, we have become theological hostage negotiators, exchanging one captive for another in the never-ending saga of trying to set people free with powerless words.

Powerless people can't stand against the wiles of the wicked one! We aren't called to be eloquent or articulate (although eloquence and articulateness are fine qualities to have if you happen to be a public speaker). We are called, commissioned, and anointed to be a dangerous, unstoppable force of love and power, flowing harmoniously in Word and Spirit! Most Christians who cry, "False prophet!" when they hear about or see supernatural manifestations can't name a real prophet who walks the earth today because they don't actually believe that prophets (or apostles) exist in our day. The early church was led by apostles and prophets, and this was the commentary on their ministry: *"These who have turned the world upside down have come here too"* (Acts 17:6 NKJV).

WE ARE ENGAGED IN THE WAR OF THE WORLDS, YET THIS WAR IS NOT BEING FOUGHT OVER TERRITORIES, COUNTRIES, OR WEALTH BUT OVER THE HEARTS OF MEN!

Today, the church is led by pastors, teachers, and a few evangelists. Yet the New Testament lists only six named teachers, one named evangelist (Philip), and not a single named pastor, while listing twenty-three named apostles and twenty-five named prophets. (There are sixty-five named prophets in the Bible if you count those in the Old Testament.) Many theologians who have never experienced the supernatural power of God and have never cast out a demon, healed the sick, or prophesied are redefining what it means to be a disciple of Jesus and to be Christlike. They are attempting to convince us that apostles and prophets were only supposed to exist in the first-century church. Furthermore, they are trying to convince us that Christians shouldn't move in miracles today.

I'm sure these theologians mean well, but this is a doctrine of demons! (See 1 Timothy 4:1.) Many powerless Bible teachers have reduced the gospel to soothe their consciences. They reason that they have never experienced a miracle, and they are believers; therefore, miracles must have ceased after the first century. Again, they may be well-meaning people, but they have reduced their doctrine to the level of their experience instead of raising their experience to match the gospel! Furthermore, the Bible gives us a timeline about how long apostles and prophets will be necessary in the body of Christ. Check it out for yourself:

> He gave some as apostles, and some as prophets, and some as evangelists, and some as pastors and teachers, for the equipping of the saints for the work of service, to the building up of the body of Christ; until we all attain to the unity of the faith, and of the knowledge of the Son of God, to a mature man, to the measure of the stature which belongs to the fullness of Christ. (Ephesians 4:11–13)

Two things stand out in this text:

1. Apostles and prophets are in place as long as pastors, teachers, and evangelists are. They all have the same "expiration date."

2. All of these ministry offices (apostles, prophets, evangelists, pastors, and teachers) are in place *until* the body of Christ (past, present, and future) comes into full maturity, measured against the fullness of Christ. So, metaphorically speaking, the body must grow until the head and the body are proportionate. We don't want a thirty-three-year-old head on a three-month-old body!

WHERE HAVE ALL THE MIRACLES GONE?

The frustration of living among a powerless people and a taunting enemy can cause us to shout, as Gideon did, *"O my lord, if the LORD is with us, why then has all this happened to us? And where are all His miracles which our fathers told us about?"* (Judges 6:13). Yet the divine greeting to Gideon still resonates with us today: *"The angel of the* LORD *appeared to him and said to him, 'The* LORD *is with you, O valiant warrior'"* (verse 12). The miracles we long for are in us! (See 1 John 4:4.) As believers, we have been called to stir up trouble for the devil and to bring hope, life, and peace to our troubled and desperate world.

THE MIRACLES WE LONG FOR ARE IN US!

A while back, late on a Sunday night during a service, I was walking through the church sanctuary, headed toward the restroom. Several hundred people were standing in long lines waiting for our prayer servants to minister to them. As I walked past the last person in line, closest to the restroom, I felt an overwhelming urge to shout over her, "Your baby is not dead but alive!" So, I stopped and went back to where the woman was standing. As soon as I came into her presence, I felt the same tremendous urge to shout over her. I had never done anything like that before; therefore, I reasoned that it must be the Lord. So, I faced her and shouted, "YOUR BABY IS NOT DEAD BUT ALIVE!" She crumbled to the floor, wailing! I went to the restroom, and when I returned, she was sitting on the floor, weeping quietly.

"Are you okay?" I gently inquired.

"I had a miscarriage this week," she said through her tears. "I just got back from the doctor's office where they did a sonogram and confirmed that my baby is dead. On Monday, they are going to do a D&C to extract the fetus from my womb. Now you are telling me it's alive!"

"Yeah, well, nothing is impossible with God," I responded, still vibrating with the presence of God.

The next Sunday morning, the same woman ran up to me, yelling excitedly, "My baby is not dead but alive! I made them do another sonogram before they removed the baby, and, lo and behold, my baby is perfectly healthy!" A few months later, she brought the newborn baby up front and showed me the miracle child!

I have literally hundreds of miracle stories like this of God touching people's lives and letting them know in tangible ways that He loves them. I like to say, "At Bethel Church, all the snakes are friendly!" Bad theology keeps people in the bondage of an inferior kingdom and can even cost them their lives. Maybe it's time for you to have your own Gideon experience and take back the land you have been promised!

13

TURNING OVER TABLES: MAD AS HELL AND ANOINTED BY HEAVEN

I am kind of a leadership junkie—I admit it. Well, okay, I am obsessed with leadership; it's true. *There, I said it!* I love books (including biographies), movies, tests, and just about anything else that has to do with leadership. I consumed *The 7 Habits of Highly Effective People*, devoured *The 8th Habit*, too, read *Good to Great* three times, and ingested the StrengthsFinder course (now called CliftonStrengths). What the heck, I even took the StrengthsFinder test! In fact, I've taken so many personality and leadership tests that I can't even remember them all. As I wrote in chapter 11, personality tests play a role in our Bethel leadership culture, and they can be beneficial if they are used appropriately. But there was a season in the global church in which many Christians began to identify and relate to each other mainly by their personality test results. (A number of them still do!) The conversations included comments like, "You know that I am an X personality type, and he is a Y personality type, so naturally...." People became so intrigued by the insights from their psychological and personality profiles that it actually became their culture. Some even went as far as assigning test profiles to biblical characters (including Jesus)! Social contracts based on these tests soon followed, and some church teams were pressured into signing contractual agreements about how they would treat one another in various circumstances. Even though most of these tests are designed to affirm *all* personality types, with everyone contributing diverse and unique gifts, the highest core value in these cultures became predictability. So, people who are instinctive, spontaneous, and/or prophetic were deemed "unsafe," "risky," and "not trustworthy."

You have probably figured out by my tone that I didn't board that train, but I sure got close enough to the track that I could hear the whistle blow and smell the smoke! During the church's "psychological experiment" (that's what I called it), rumors that people like me were "unsafe" began to circulate throughout the body of Christ. I spent countless hours trying to understand how we were "unsafe" so that I/we could change. Some of my personal conversations with people went something like this:

They would say, "Well, you are very direct with people, and you let them know what you are thinking."

"Do I raise my voice or act disrespectfully in anyway?" I would question.

"No, you're just scary! People feel like you can see into their souls, and it makes them feel very uncomfortable."

After this, our conversations would usually digress to my being contrasted with some mild-mannered person whom they wanted me to emulate. It seemed like, when I wasn't being compared to someone's pet lamb, I was being lectured to about the gentle nature of Jesus. Of course, there was truth to some of their accusations, as we all certainly have areas in our lives in which we need to grow.

I finally engaged a leadership coach so I could help myself and all the "scary" people like me make the transition to wholeness. His counsel went something like this: "Mr. Vallotton, your personality test reveals that you have an extremely dominant nature. Here are my recommendations for ways that you should manage yourself." His suggestions centered on things like learning diplomacy, being more patient, acquiring listening skills, and so forth. Again, we all need to grow in these areas, but it felt more like I was being domesticated, neutered, and/or tamed than trained. Personally, I believe that Christians were born for the wild, but it felt like we were being prepared for the zoo. In fact, in my opinion, the church was becoming a zoo—or at least a wildlife preserve. Metaphorically speaking, the natural instincts of the lion—hunting its own prey, protecting the pride, and leading with fierce courage—were no longer valued. They were being replaced with skills like learning to sit on a stool, jumping through hoops, and roaring on key. The church was becoming a corporate culture: predictable, boring, riskless, and subdued. The zookeepers loved it, but I hated it!

JUNGLE ETHICS

Now, before we go nuts here and incite a riot against the "pastoral people" or let the raging bulls loose to trample the "religious Pharisees" in the halls of our churches, I want to make it clear that even lions in their natural habitat observe jungle ethics! What I mean is that nobility, honor, and respect are all part of a healthy wilderness environment. So, life in the kingdom isn't a free-for-all! Furthermore, I have personally had it with people who spiritualize their own dysfunction by finding some verse in the Bible that seems to validate their rudeness, brokenness, or mean-spiritedness. Although I don't want us to be reduced by the whip of the lion tamer, I certainly do believe in living a life of true nobility and excellent character. But a social contract or a policy manual, while it may be necessary, won't ever achieve nobility. Nobility is the fruit of the true love of Jesus gushing from the wellsprings of the lives of His people. It is courageous love expressed in sacrifice, humility, and generosity. Yet there is also a fierce love that subdues its enemies—such as sin, hatred, prejudice, and deception—with unbridled passion and strategic yet reckless abandon.

NOBILITY IS THE FRUIT OF THE TRUE LOVE OF JESUS GUSHING FROM THE WELLSPRINGS OF THE LIVES OF HIS PEOPLE.

WHO IS YOUR DADDY?

Here is the unnerving question that began to press against my soul during that season—a question that no one seemed to be asking: What is the standard by which we should be measuring ourselves? I mean, personality profiles are sometimes used by people in an attempt to shape us into those who "fit" into society and become "congenial contributors" to our communities. We certainly want to be good citizens who love the people around us. But is that it? Is our goodness measured by how much favor we can muster in society? Is the pinnacle of the temple of godliness "spiritual eunuchs" who are trusted in society because their natural desire to consummate their own legacy has been gelded? Would you really rather be safe than sorry? Is Christianity all about being nice, safe, soft-spoken, and non-offensive? Again, who should we be modeling our life after? Who can we look to who would settle this turmoil in our souls?

BECOMING LIKE JESUS

I think the standard answer is Jesus! Isn't it the goal of Christians to become Christlike? Then, the million-dollar question is this: What is Christ like? As Bill Johnson often says, "Jesus is perfect theology; therefore, if you don't see what you believe in the life of Jesus, you have reason to question its legitimacy." In fact, the great apostle Paul put it like this: "*We all, with unveiled face, beholding as in a mirror the glory of the Lord, are being transformed into the same image from glory to glory, just as from the Lord, the Spirit*" (2 Corinthians 3:18).

Thus, if the supreme goal of following Jesus is to become like Him (to become Christlike), it's paramount that what we think about Him is actually true, or, shall we say, "the whole truth, and nothing but the truth, so help me God!" The weird thing is that the twenty-first-century church has disguised Jesus so well that He has essentially vanished among the politically correct crowd and is virtually missing in action in modern culture. Part of the challenge is that we tend to gravitate toward a one-dimensional perspective of our Lord that is sort of user-friendly. But what about the Jesus of the Bible? Was He really a soft-spoken, gentle pacifist who spent most of His time kissing babies' foreheads and holding love feasts?

Personally, I think we have mistaken our Lord for a Buddhist monk humming a meaningless chant while holding an incense canister. Yet the Gospels paint quite a different picture of Jesus. The apostle John recorded this scene:

> *Jesus went up to Jerusalem. And He found in the temple those who were selling oxen and sheep and doves, and the moneychangers seated at their tables. And He made a scourge of cords, and drove them all out of the temple, with the sheep and the oxen; and He poured out the coins of the money changers and overturned their tables; and to those who were selling the doves He said, "Take these things away; stop making My Father's house a place of business." His disciples remembered*

that it was written, "Zeal for Your house will consume me."

(John 2:13–17)

Did you catch the line *"He made a scourge of cords"*? Jesus made a scourge, which is a whip used for punishment, and He used it to whip the people who were doing business in the temple!

PATIENCE OR TOLERANCE?

Love is patient—but tolerance is not the same thing as patience. Tolerance must be bathed in wisdom and strategically offered in a way that creates a highway to wholeness. Otherwise, whatever is tolerated becomes the culture. Jesus has a lot to say about the fine line between patience and tolerance. Here is a case in point: He pulls no punches in His discourse with the church in Thyatira on their inability to confront a wicked woman in their congregation. Here is His exhortation:

> *To the angel of the church in Thyatira write: The Son of God, who has eyes like a flame of fire, and His feet are like burnished bronze, says this: "I know your deeds, and your love and faith and service and perseverance, and that your deeds of late are greater than at first. But I have this against you, that you tolerate the woman Jezebel, who calls herself a prophetess, and she teaches and leads My bond-servants astray so that they commit acts of immorality and eat things sacrificed to idols. I gave her time to repent, and she does not want to repent of her immorality. Behold, I will throw her on a bed of sickness, and those who commit adultery with her into great tribulation, unless they repent of her deeds. And I will kill her children with pestilence, and all the churches will know that I am He who searches the minds and hearts; and I will give to each one of you according to your deeds."* (Revelation 2:18–23)

Wow, the judgment Jesus proclaimed against Jezebel is pretty intense! Yet what's even more shocking to me is our Lord's commentary on the church in Thyatira: *"You tolerate the woman Jezebel."* They didn't

celebrate her—they just tolerated her. But whatever we tolerate dominates! The outcome of letting the harlot Jezebel attend their church was
that she led their congregation into immorality and idolatry. This very
closely mirrors the attitude of much of the modern church today. We
want sinners to be welcome in our churches so that they can hear the
gospel and be saved. Therefore, we water down the gospel so that nobody
is offended, but, consequently, nobody feels convicted either. In fact, in
the name of *love*, we actually embrace the immoral lifestyles of fornication, adultery, homosexuality, and so on as normal, healthy expressions
of Christianity. But the consequence of embracing people who are living
immoral lifestyles without requiring them to repent from their sin to
follow Jesus is that they suck many more people into the vortex of their
immorality. Ultimately, this leads to virtueless people finding their way
into leadership and polluting the mindset of the masses.

WHATEVER WE TOLERATE DOMINATES!

LEAVING THE PIG FARM

The story of the prodigal son comes to mind again here because the
father has deep love for his wayward younger son, who is living a life of
immorality. There is so much wisdom in the father's approach to his
son. Let's revisit the story, which we talked about briefly in chapter 10.
A farmer has two sons, the younger of which is wayward, rebellious,
and worldly. The younger son decides to exit his dad's house with his
portion of the inheritance. He parties it up with prostitutes and pimps,
and soon he is stone broke. Half starving to death, he winds up working
at a pig farm, slopping hogs. It's actually quite ironic that he gets stuck
at a pig farm because Jews in those days (as is the case today among
Orthodox Jews) weren't supposed to eat pork; it was unclean under

the law. So, the pig farm becomes a prophetic monument to the boy's misery: a son in rebellion living an unclean life, feeding unclean animals—and all because he had entertained unclean thoughts in his very clean father's house! In the midst of his misery, the son has an epiphany: "What the heck am doing at this pig palace when I could be living at my father's farm?" So, he comes to himself and heads home. (See Luke 15:11–32.)

What can we learn from the prodigal's pilgrimage? First of all, we must embrace his father's faith for reconciliation, which is demonstrated by his expectation of his son's return. He is able to meet his son in his field of dreams because he is watching in earnest expectation. I think it's important to reinforce here that the father had faith for his son's return—for his repentance, his change of heart. As we noted earlier, the father wasn't guided by unsanctified mercy, accepting his son's sinful lifestyle in order to woo the boy homeward. And his son respected his father's nobility and understood that he couldn't bring his immoral lifestyle to the father's farm, knowing that prostitutes and pigs were unwelcome there. No, instead, there is an unspoken understanding in the story that the son must acknowledge his sin and forsake a lifestyle of perversion in exchange for regaining his family's noble virtues.

We have seen that sometimes our love for people is not rooted in faith for their restoration. Instead, in fear, we undermine the process of repentance, circumventing the journey by renegotiating the terms of reconciliation. Metaphorically speaking (and at the risk of sounding rude), we turn the farm into a whorehouse to entice prodigals to return home because we reason that it's our holy standard that is keeping them away. Furthermore, we lack faith in the Holy Spirit's ability to convict them of their sin and give them the grace they need to change! Somehow, in our zeal, we mistakenly believe that God's goal is to get them back in the building when, in fact, God's goal is repentance—to change their way of thinking and agree with His noble lifestyle. The apostle Paul said it best: *"Do you think lightly of the riches of His kindness and tolerance and*

patience, not knowing that the kindness of God leads you to repentance?"
(Romans 2:4). Let me point out once more that God's kindness leads to
repentance, which results in restoration. But promoting reentry without
repentance isn't restoration; it's human sympathy, not God-ordained
compassion.

The wayward son's repentance is evidenced by his confession: *"Father,
I have sinned against heaven and in your sight; I am no longer worthy to be
called your son"* (Luke 15:21). The confession of sin is paramount in the
reentry process because it's the catalyst for *grace,* which gives the power
to change. As mentioned in chapter 7, "Failing Successfully," the apostle
John expressed it like this: *"If we say that we have no sin, we are deceiving
ourselves and the truth is not in us. If we confess our sins, He is faithful and
righteous to forgive us our sins and to cleanse us from all unrighteousness"*
(1 John 1:8–9). The challenge is that you can't separate confession from
being cleansed from unrighteousness. Therefore, if we normalize sin
and refuse to admit that what we are doing is wrong, we undermine the
power of *grace,* which is the supernatural ability to change.

The tendency of churches to try to reconcile people to themselves
(telling them, "You're okay just the way you are") instead of helping
them be reconciled to God (where they will find their true purpose and
worth) has undermined their congregations' journeys to wholeness and
reduced people to spineless sinners—powerless individuals who remain
shackled to their addictions, imprisoned by their ever-changing passions. For many leaders, the ability to share a message with their congregation without offending or convicting anyone is viewed as an art that
must be mastered. But there is no such thing as godly love without conviction. Love is loyal; therefore, when we are disloyal, we feel convicted.
Love is pure; so, being impure causes conviction. Love always tells the
truth; thus, lying brings conviction. Love always hopes; so, hopelessness
breeds conviction.

I must love you more than my convictions, but I can't love you *instead
of* my convictions. As I pointed out earlier, Jesus forgave the woman who

was caught in adultery. *Yes*, that's true, but He also loved her enough to exhort her, *"Go your way. From now on sin no more"* (John 8:11 NASB77).

Becoming a virtueless cesspool so that dirty people (all of us get dirty at times) don't feel bad about being dirty undermines our divine call to help filthy people become clean. For instance, have you ever, without realizing it, washed off a tabletop with dirty water, only to discover that, after it dried, it was filthier than before you cleaned it? It's not that Christians are better than anybody else; it's just that we have acknowledged our sin and our need for a Savior. In other words, we know we have a problem, and we've allowed God to provide the solution. But there is no solution until we acknowledge our problem. It's impossible to help someone with a problem that they don't believe they have. Certain sins might be common (and/or politically correct), but sin is never normal. Furthermore, as I have emphasized, making sin acceptable undermines any chance for a real resolution. Leaving people hopelessly stuck in their sin isn't loving—it's ridiculous, cruel, reckless, and irresponsible. Jesus died to save sinners *from* sin, not *to* sin!

OVERCOME WITH *ZEŌ*

Compassion is very important in our lives, and it must be the central theme of everything we do. But compassion alone is often not enough to make a difference. When Jesus drove the moneychangers out of the temple, turning over their tables and chasing them with a whip, He wasn't overcome with compassion—He was filled with zeal! (See John 2:17.) The Greek root word for *"zeal"* in this verse is *zeō*. *Zeō* means "to boil," "to be hot," or "to be fervent"![22] At the risk of sounding like I am promoting rage or violence, I must point out that Jesus was overcome with *zeō*—and He was done being passive with the moneychangers. His blood was boiling, and they were about to get a piece of His mind! Can you imagine the disciples telling Him, "Jesus, You need to chillax...calm

---

22. "G2204–zeō, Strong's Greek Lexicon (KJV)," Blue Letter Bible, accessed June 24, 2025, https://www.blueletterbible.org/lexicon/g2204/kjv/tr/0-1/; "2204. Zeó," Bible Lexicon, Bible Hub, https://biblehub.com/greek/2204.htm.

down…or people are going to misunderstand You"? No *way*! Jesus loves people, but compassion must be accompanied by zeal in order to see real change.

Nobody enjoys being misunderstood, but anyone who does anything great will be; it just goes with the territory. Jesus's ministry was steeped in misunderstandings; and, frankly, sometimes He seemed to rather enjoy it—like the time He gave His "You must eat My flesh and drink My blood" message. That day, He preached His multitude of followers all the way down to twelve! And the disciples stayed only because they had nowhere else to go. (See John 6:35–69.) Does it trouble you that Jesus didn't try to explain Himself to the crowd? It does me! I mean, a few minutes of diplomacy might have gone a long way in that situation. But He simply refused to explain Himself, choosing instead to let the crowds disperse in confusion rather than follow Him by persuasion. "Why?" you may ask. I am not sure, but it's apparent that God tests our hearts with mysteries and misunderstandings. Can you imagine what the posts would have been like if there had been social media in Jesus's day? How would Jesus have been described by His detractors? I love what Winston Churchill said about responding to criticism: "You will never reach your destination if you stop and throw stones at every dog that barks."[23]

FOLLOWING IN HIS FOOTSTEPS

Unlike Jesus, many people today are obsessed with wooing people with sophistication or wowing them with articulation. Again, we must be motivated by love that is rooted in compassion and not judgment. But it's important to realize that, although Jesus hung out with sinners and went to their parties—and ultimately died for all sinners—He never compromised His message or His life to make them feel welcome. Who

---

23. Winston Churchill, "Winston S. Churchill: Quotes," Goodreads, https://www. goodreads.com/quotes/407062-you-will-never-reach-your-destination-if-you-stop-and.

can forget Jesus's simple message on lust, which He spoke during the Sermon on the Mount?

> You have heard that it was said, "You shall not commit adultery," but I say to you that everyone who looks at a woman with lust for her has already committed adultery with her in his heart. If your right eye makes you stumble, tear it out and throw it from you; for it is better for you to lose one of the parts of your body, than for your whole body to be thrown into hell. If your right hand makes you stumble, cut it off and throw it from you; for it is better for you to lose one of the parts of your body, than for your whole body to go into hell.
>
> (Matthew 5:27–30)

IF WE ARE GOING TO BECOME
CHRISTLIKE, WE HAVE TO EMBRACE
THE AUTHENTIC GOSPEL THAT GIVES
PEOPLE SOMETHING WORTH DYING FOR
SO THAT THE PAIN OF CRUCIFIXION IS
SWALLOWED UP BY THE JOY OF A PURE
HEART AND A CLEAN CONSCIENCE.

Jesus didn't dumb down his message to please the crowd. He was a radical revolutionary who continually challenged the multitudes to lay down their life of sin for a greater purpose. If we are going to become Christlike, we have to embrace the authentic gospel that gives people something worth dying for so that the pain of crucifixion is swallowed up by the joy of a pure heart and a clean conscience. Modern-day Pharisees, who are soothing their consciences with religion and are measuring the impact of their lives by the size of the fans and followers they amass on their social-media pages, will always be offended by the call to a holy life. Similarly, the modern-day moneychangers who are more concerned about the business of ministry than about the souls of men have a consumer–customer relationship with the crowd. Their "customer is always right" core value tests the direction of the wind to determine the stances they take. Yet Jesus is certainly not your mild-mannered reporter! He is a bull in the fake-and-fantasy china shop. Sinners looking for freedom and deliverance were attracted to His honest and authentic message of repentance, which liberated them from their life of shame and guilt, and wooed them into the palace of divine possibilities. On the other hand, people who were looking to justify their lifestyle of compromise, sin, or rebellion loathed our Master's ministry.

If we are determined to follow in the footsteps of our Lord, then seasons of righteous indignation will rise from our spirit as we combat religious Pharisees and opportunists who use their perverse business shrewdness to take clever advantage of weak, vulnerable people. Our call to righteous nobility reminds me of the Bible character named Job. Job was a noble man whose righteous exploits famously attracted the attention of the devil himself. (See Job 1:6–12.) Job was an Old Testament reformer who used his wealth and his favor to care for the vulnerable and to take a stand against wickedness. Here is a portion of Job's own observation of the impact that his life had on the earth:

The voice of the nobles was hushed, and their tongue stuck to their palate. For when the ear heard, it called me blessed, and when the eye saw, it gave witness of me, because I delivered the poor who cried for help, and the orphan who had no helper. The blessing of the one ready to perish came upon me, and I made the widow's heart sing for joy. I put on righteousness, and it clothed me; my justice was like a robe and a turban. I was eyes to the blind and feet to the lame. I was a father to the needy, and I investigated the case which I did not know. I broke the jaws of the wicked and snatched the prey from his teeth.

(Job 29:10–17)

This is our call, our divine privilege, and our mandate! When noble believers come face-to-face with workers of wickedness or the schemes of the devil, it should rouse table-flipping *zeō* (zeal) in our spirits. Righteous indignation will boil over in the depth of our being as we encounter demonic devices that are postured to destroy the people whom Jesus died to save. Like a father who encounters an intruder trying to harm his family in his home, he becomes "mad as hell but anointed by heaven"! So, the righteous must vigilantly stand against the deeds of the devil as zeal for God's house consumes us!

Remember, standing strong doesn't mean avoiding the storms of life, running from conflict, or sitting quietly while the enemy ravages our loved ones. It means that we are weatherproof—that we are *all-weather people*. We were created to thrive in every season of life! Like Jesus, we know how to sit quietly in the face of accusation—not out of fear but out of wisdom. Yet we also recognize when to step out of the crowd and confront a situation head-on because we are equipped with the armor of God, which means we were built for battle.

14

CHOOSE YOUR
ENEMIES WELL

Jesus said, *"Love your enemies"* (Matthew 5:44; Luke 6:27, 35). It's important to have enemies because they are one of the signs that we are living a life worth resisting. An ineffective or complacent life isn't worth opposing. Yet, in the twenty-first century, there are so many unproductive ways to make enemies that rob us of our energy and steal our capacity, leaving us with no divine purpose or reward. These days, it seems like the devil sets our barns on fire, and we rush to the fires, not realizing that our houses are being pillaged, our children abducted, and our marriages destroyed.

I doubt there was another time in modern history when this was more prevalent than during the COVID-19 and social-justice seasons. It felt like we ran from fire to fire—accusing one another, frustrated by the restrictions, looking for someone to blame, and living to find a path out of our pain. Personally, I made more enemies during those two years than I had made in my entire lifetime; but the troubling reality is that most of my "righteous stands" had no divine purpose or eternal reward, and they made enemies out of people whom I am called to befriend. Today, I look back with regret and wish I had stayed the course of my calling!

My frustration grew every week as the situation intensified. People hated each other because they would or wouldn't get vaccinated. Others were livid because a church or business did or did not follow the governmental COVID-19 mandates. Finally, one Sunday morning, in the midst of the COVID chaos, I got so fed up with the hatred and accusations flying around that I shouted in my message, "If you want to die on the pro-mask or anti-mask mountain, feel free to do so. If you want to sacrifice your life for an anti-vax or pro-vax stance, knock yourself out! *But* don't drag me up on that mountain because I am not going to give my life for something that has *no* eternal value!" That statement galvanized my leadership core values and thus determined where I would spend my energy for the rest of the COVID crisis. The following week, I got vaccinated, and I stood up and shared my vax status with our congregation. I didn't get vaccinated for the virus; I took the shot to silence the growing perspective that the leaders of Bethel Church were anti-vax activists. Certainly, some were, but I didn't want our church to be aligned with a cause that wasn't demonstrated by the life of Jesus, taught by the apostles, or found in the Scriptures.

I respect people who have a different perspective and thus take another stance. I love people who care enough about life that they find something they believe is worth spending their energy on. But, personally, I want to choose my own battles and engage the enemies I am called and equipped to defeat. Sometimes, refusing to engage a taunting giant is one of the wisest acts of courage.

I think my passion for picking the right fight was instilled in me as a teenager because I grew up during the Vietnam War era. That was a time when men and women came home in body bags by the thousands; children were made fatherless and motherless, while dads and moms wept over caskets draped with the American flag. Sadly, all this took place in the backdrop of a largely ungrateful nation, whose anti-war protestors burned our flag in the streets of our cities.

So, the question of the hour is "Why?" or "For what reason?" What was accomplished during that time? I am so thankful for people who are willing to give their lives to protect our country, our freedom, and our people. Yet I find myself personally plagued by the haunting question, "For what or for whom am I willing to die?" I wonder, "Is the cause noble—something I am called and equipped to engage in?" Furthermore, if I fight *this* enemy, what would it keep me from doing instead? I am not omnipresent, so I can't be everywhere at once. As noble people, we are tasked with determining the priorities of our life and death.

AS NOBLE PEOPLE, WE ARE TASKED WITH DETERMINING THE PRIORITIES OF OUR LIFE AND DEATH.

FIGHT FOR VICTORY AND RACE TO WIN

I can't count how many funerals I've been to where the commentary on the deceased has gone something like this: "Johnny got along with everyone; he had no enemies." Now, let me be clear, I don't think our battle is against flesh and blood (see Ephesians 6:12), and I do believe we should love everyone, friend or foe—*but*, again, if we are living up to our full potential, we will attract resistance from people. The apostle Paul challenged his beloved disciple Timothy, "*Fight the good fight of faith; take hold of the eternal life to which you were called, and you made the good confession in the presence of many witnesses"* (1 Timothy 6:12). At the end of his own life, he wrote to Timothy once more about the *"good fight"* of faith: *"I have fought the good fight, I have finished the course, I have kept the faith"* (2 Timothy 4:7). Paul exhorted the Corinthians with these powerful words: *"Do you not know that those who run in a race all run, but only one receives the prize? Run in such a way that you may win"* (1 Corinthians 9:24). Life in Christ was never meant to be a "row, row, row your boat gently down the stream" journey of ease and comfort! We each have been given a fight to fight and a race to run. Furthermore, we are to fight for victory and race to win!

FINDING YOUR PURPOSE IN THE FRAY

Often, we discover the thing we are born for when we engage in a conflict. I remember one of those defining moments in my life. One of the leadership couples I oversaw at Bethel was in my office, sharing their deep concern over the moral and economic condition of our state of California. "We want to move someplace like Texas that's morally conservative and business friendly," they explained. They rattled off several examples of how the culture of California had become a cesspool of immorality, impurity, and debauchery, with which I completely agreed. Yet the longer they talked, the more incensed I became—not at them but with the condition of the state of our union. (I was born in California, as were my parents, my kids, and all twelve of my grandkids). I finally interrupted them, and, leaning toward them, I blurted out, "Nobody is going to drive me out of my land! Nobody! This is the land of my forefathers, the place of my promise and the estate of my legacy! I will not be intimidated into silence or punished into powerlessness. I refuse to become a passive pundit of a demised society, or a docile puppet bowing to the demands of a confused and demented people! I am, by the grace of Christ, a man of God, and I have been called and commissioned to shift the culture of California toward the King and His kingdom!"

They both just sat there, staring at me. I sort of shocked myself because I didn't know that was stewing in my spirit. A minute later, I leaned back in my chair and offered a half-hearted apology. I was truly sorry that they had encountered the wrath of my frustration, as they certainly didn't deserve it, but I was intrigued by this sudden explosion of passion, forced to the surface of my soul by their desire to retreat to a safer state.

This experience reminds me of Saul, who, as we talked about in a previous chapter, was anointed by Samuel the prophet to be the king of Israel. I would say that being commissioned as Israel's first-ever king was a pretty big deal. But Saul didn't want to be king, so, after the commissioning, he literally went back to farming—*until* this happened:

> *Now Nahash the Ammonite came up and besieged Jabesh-gilead;*
> *and all the men of Jabesh said to Nahash, "Make a covenant with us*
> *and we will serve you." But Nahash the Ammonite said to them, "I*
> *will make it with you on this condition, that I will gouge out the right*
> *eye of every one of you, thus I will make it a reproach on all Israel."*
> *The elders of Jabesh said to him, "Let us alone for seven days, that*
> *we may send messengers throughout the territory of Israel. Then, if*
> *there is no one to deliver us, we will come out to you." Then the mes-*
> *sengers came to Gibeah of Saul and spoke these words in the hear-*
> *ing of the people, and all the people lifted up their voices and wept.*
> *Now behold, Saul was coming from the field behind the oxen, and he*
> *said, "What is the matter with the people that they weep?" So, they*
> *related to him the words of the men of Jabesh. Then the Spirit of God*
> *came upon Saul mightily when he heard these words, and he became*
> *very angry. He took a yoke of oxen and cut them in pieces, and sent*
> *them throughout the territory of Israel by the hand of messengers,*
> *saying, "Whoever does not come out after Saul and after Samuel, so*
> *shall it be done to his oxen." Then the dread of the* LORD *fell on the*
> *people, and they came out as one man.* (1 Samuel 11:1–7)

Saul went to war against the Ammonites and defeated them, which freed his people and solidified his kingship. (See verses 8–14.) It's important to point out here that the war that was meant to defeat Saul actually revealed the greatness in him, both to himself and to the nation.

As I mentioned earlier in this book, the same thing happened in the life of David. As a shepherd boy, David was anointed king in secret by Samuel, but his greatness was exposed to the Israelites when they encountered Goliath. The giant taunted them relentlessly for forty days until the boy wonder killed him with a rock and rose to fame overnight!

The battles that we face will often reveal the work that God is doing in the secret spaces of our hearts. God is always at work in us, but life is so daily that it's common to be clueless about the extensive nature of God's work within our inner man. Furthermore, the people we do life with have become so familiar with our humanity that it's hard for them to discern the supernatural nature of what's growing inside us. Consequently, it often takes a crisis to unleash the intensity of the wondrous work growing in the soil of our soul. It's in crisis that we shed the garments of the common man and reveal the cape of the superhero—who was born for battle, equipped for combat, and destined to win!

When we retreat in the face of battle, we let our enemy live another day in vicious victory, which further perpetuates tragedy in our lives and in the lives of people whom we love. But when we step into the fray, be it with trepidation or with triumph, we send this clear message and clarion call to all hostiles: *"Not on my watch!"*

KNOW YOUR ENEMY

Someone once said, "All that evil needs to triumph is for good people to do nothing!" Yet I think the truth is deeper than that: I think good people need to do the *right thing*, not just *something*. In fact, when righteous people do the wrong thing or the stupid thing, it often deepens the resolve of evil people, entrenching their negative impact on society.

Courage and boldness are important character qualities because, without them, it's nearly impossible to make any lasting impact on the world. For example, God told Joshua to be *"strong and courageous"* three times in the first chapter of the book bearing his name (see Joshua 1:6–7, 9), and the phrase is used in various forms thirteen times in the Old Testament. In nearly every instance, this phrase is used as an exhortation for someone to press in to win a battle and overcome an enemy. But, in my observation, the body of Christ, generally speaking, doesn't lack courage; we lack preparation and strategy. We are often on the right side of something that we know little to nothing about. Therefore, thinking people discount our position—not because we are wrong but because we are uninformed.

The apostle Peter exhorted us, *"Therefore, prepare your minds for action"* (1 Peter 1:13). Solomon gave similar advice: *"A wise man is strong, and a man of knowledge increases power. For by wise guidance, you will wage war, and in abundance of counselors there is victory"* (Proverbs 24:5–6). He also advised, *"Without consultation, plans are frustrated, but with many counselors they succeed"* (Proverbs 15:22). I can't tell you how many times I've heard a Christian debating an issue with an unbeliever—and the believer sounds like one of the characters out of the movie *Dumb and Dumber!* Or, as Forrest Gump put it, "Stupid is as stupid does!" I often want to run away and hide, or pretend I don't know them.

COUNTING THE COST

Our life in Christ was supposed to begin with an internal evaluation of the cost of discipleship and a strategy for finishing the race for eternity. Case in point: Jesus was discussing the cost of discipleship with the crowd. He reminded them that following Him would cost them everything. He challenged them to evaluate whether they had what it took to successfully build their life in Christ. Furthermore, did they believe that they were strong enough to engage the enemy of their souls without losing themselves in the fight? Here is a portion of that conversation:

[Jesus said,] *For which one of you, when he wants to build a tower, does not first sit down and calculate the cost to see if he has enough to complete it? Otherwise, when he has laid a foundation and is not able to finish, all who observe it begin to ridicule him, saying, "This man began to build and was not able to finish." Or what king, when he sets out to meet another king in battle, will not first sit down and consider whether he is strong enough with ten thousand men to encounter the one coming against him with twenty thousand? Or else, while the other is still far away, he sends a delegation and asks for terms of peace. So then, none of you can be My disciple who does not give up all his own possessions.* (Luke 14:28–33)

OUR LIFE IN CHRIST WAS SUPPOSED TO BEGIN WITH AN INTERNAL EVALUATION OF THE COST OF DISCIPLESHIP AND A STRATEGY FOR FINISHING THE RACE FOR ETERNITY.

Personally, I find it hard to imagine someone sitting down with a piece of paper and writing down the pros and cons of following Jesus. Or a person evaluating the battle that will ensue against them if they leave the path of sin and take the highway of holiness. But this type of self-evaluation is vital for our faith. In other words, we must ask ourselves questions like these: "If Christ is on my side, do I have what it takes to win the war assigned to me?" "Am I prepared to pay the ultimate cost of 'finishing the tower' of my salvation?" These were some of the points Jesus was making when He addressed the crowd.

So, here is my observation: if our salvation is supposed to begin with a strategy, then why do we often lack any kind of strategic plan for

victory in our daily lives? There are so many battles that we are commissioned to fight, but it's not enough to engage an enemy—we must
also be prepared to *win*. Some Christians struggle their whole life with
the same sin—lust, selfishness, violence, pride, immorality, lying, fear,
porn...the list goes on and on—with literally no forward motion! It's
hard to righteously choose to fight an enemy that is around me when I
haven't won the war within me. It may be common for believers to jump
into the fray before they are ready, but *it is not okay!* We need to develop
a "spiritategy" (a Spirit-led strategy) to win the battle within us so that
we are fortified for the war around us!

WAR OR PEACE?

But Jesus wasn't done with His "war-side" chat! He exhorted, *"Do
not think that I came to bring peace on the earth"* (Matthew 10:34). When
we read this, it's easy to think, "Okay, but I was sort of hoping You were
going to bring peace; that was Your jam, Lord!" Yet Jesus went on to say:

> *I did not come to bring peace, but a sword. For I came to set a
> man against his father, and a daughter against her mother, and a
> daughter-in-law against her mother-in-law; and a man's enemies
> will be the members of his household. He who loves father or mother
> more than Me is not worthy of Me; and he who loves son or daughter
> more than Me is not worthy of Me. And he who does not take his
> cross and follow after Me is not worthy of Me. He who has found
> his life will lose it, and he who has lost his life for My sake will find
> it.* (Matthew 10:34–39)

Let's be honest: no one puts these declarations on their refrigerator.
I mean, you never see these Scriptures printed on a beautiful picture of
Jesus hanging over someone's fireplace mantel. Yet, there they are in the
Bible, in bright red "Jesus letters," just one chapter before the famous
"Come to Me, all who are weary and heavy-laden, and I will give you rest"
(Matthew 11:28) verse. The truth is, if we give ourselves completely to

Christ, many people will choose to make us their enemy, even people we dearly love. Of course, not everyone hates us for the cause of Christ; often, people dislike us because of our attitudes and/or actions. It's up to us to display the love of Jesus to everyone—friend or foe.

Some people may choose to make me their enemy…but my strategy for them is largely to ignore their accusations and their taunting. I do my best to not fight with people; it's usually a colossal waste of time and energy. The fight I am talking about isn't aimed at humans (although they will often join the fray); it's a war against a dark kingdom, led by an evil prince. This prince sucks people into his cesspool of wickedness, brands their consciences with the hot iron of shame, steals their innocence, and incarcerates their souls. These are the battles I want to proactively choose to go after with everything I am. How about you? What war are you dying to win?

15

THE OPENING
OF A NEW ERA

I love the story of David and Goliath, and we have visited it a couple of times in this book already. But I am so inspired by T.D. Jakes's insight into the story. I once heard him put it like this in an online sermon: "God didn't send Goliath to David to kill him; He sent him to reveal him." It's true! If it hadn't been for Goliath, David might never have become the king of Israel. As I emphasized in the previous chapter, many of us are missing the point of our problems and are being crushed by the very thing that has been sent to uncover the king or queen within us. To stand strong, we need to allow God to reveal what He's up to inside us and discover what He wants to do through us.

RIDICULOUS BATTLE PLANS

The truth is, the enemy often knows our destiny better than we do. Let's go back to the story of Gideon, who was called to free the Israelites from the Midianites, who had been oppressing them for decades. You can read the entire story in Judges 6–7.

Gideon was a farmer, not a fighter; furthermore, the Israelites were severely outnumbered and outgunned. So dire was the situation that the Lord had to send Gideon an angel, who called him a *"valiant warrior"* (Judges 6:12), to get him off the couch of complacency. When Gideon finally agreed to lead Israel in battle against overwhelming odds, God gave him a ridiculous battle plan: First, He instructed Gideon to send all the soldiers home who were afraid; and, just like that, Gideon's army shrank from thirty-two thousand men to ten thousand soldiers! But wait—God wasn't done pruning! God called Gideon back to the heavenly situation room and insisted that only the soldiers who drank water from the river by lapping like dogs could be in Gideon's army. Well, that minor criteria shrank his army from ten thousand men to three hundred dog lappers! But God wasn't finished implementing His outrageous strategy; next, He instructed Gideon to equip those remaining men with three hundred torches, jars, and trumpets. Did you notice anything missing from the equipment list—like swords, spears, and bows?

Then, God revealed the battle strategy: "Okay Gideon, here is the plan: wait until nighttime, and then you and your men go down to the outskirts of the Midianites' camp. Next, I want you to simultaneously blow the trumpets and break the jars—then quickly hold up the torches, shouting, *'For the LORD and for Gideon.'"* If I had been Gideon, I would been like, "Really? This is Your plan? This is a suicide mission." Gideon, of course, is terrified; I mean, who wouldn't be?

So, that night, God confronted Gideon and said, "If you are afraid, go down to the enemy's camp with your servant and hear what they are saying about you!" Gideon arrived at the enemy's camp just in time to hear one of the soldiers recounting a dream that he had:

> "Behold, I had a dream; a loaf of barley bread was tumbling into the camp of Midian, and it came to the tent and struck it so that it fell, and turned it upside down so that the tent lay flat." His friend replied, "This is nothing less than the sword of Gideon the son of Joash, a man of Israel; God has given Midian and all the camp into his hand."
>
> (Judges 7:13–14)

Gideon went on to miraculously defeat the Midianites and free Israel from its archenemy.

THE MORAL OF THE STORY

This story is powerful for many reasons, but the fact that the enemy actually knew that Gideon was destined to destroy them is mind-blowing! Of course, the point of this story, for our purposes, is to illustrate how insightful the devil is concerning the plans of God for our lives. All of us experience trials, but it rarely occurs to us that the enemy may well be the one who is resisting us at our place of purpose and providence.

In chapter 6, we discussed the fact that the way out of trials that are rooted in spiritual warfare is to submit to God and resist the devil so that he will flee from us. We also learned that we may experience trials as God tests and strengthens our faith, builds our character, and releases our destiny. There is always a divinely placed giant in every promised land! Remember the "giants" in the story of Moses? Moses sent twelve spies into the promised land to develop a plan for the Israelites to inhabit their inheritance. But ten spies came back with a bad report: "*There we saw the giants…; and we were like grasshoppers in our own sight, and so we were in their sight*" (Numbers 13:33 NKJV). Consequently, the Israelites became terrified and refused to conquer the land. Ultimately, all the Israelites who had been delivered out of Egypt and had miraculously crossed the Red

Sea on dry land died in the wilderness, except for Joshua and Caleb. The irony of the situation is that, forty years later, when the children born in the wilderness finally entered the promised land, they didn't encounter a single giant for about three hundred and seventy years, and then a fifteen-year-old boy (David) killed him with a rock. (Some might point out here that Caleb went after the giants in the promised land. He certainly went after the sons of Anak [see, for example, Joshua 11:21; 15:13–14], who might have been giants. But there isn't a single battle recounted in the Bible in which Caleb killed a giant.)

GIANTS AND GRASSHOPPERS

The size of a giant is often determined not so much by their height or strength but by the influence they have on the way we view ourselves and God in their presence. The size of a man can be determined by the size of the problem it takes to discourage him. So, if Satan sends a small demon after you, he has very little respect for your authority or power. Therefore, the more he fears you, the more he resists you!

Furthermore, the strength we build in the fight against our enemy is necessary for us to stay in our land of promise. Overcoming the obstacles of life is the very thing that prepares us for our divine destiny. It toughens us up as warriors, builds calluses on our hands, and strengthens our spiritual muscles to thrive in the fray. This principle is demonstrated in God's strategy for the Israelites to inhabit the promised land. He said, *"I will not drive them out before you in a single year, that the land may not become desolate and the beasts of the field become too numerous for you. I will drive them out before you little by little, until you become fruitful and take possession of the land"* (Exodus 23:29–30). The Lord allowed the enemy to live in the land until His people's leadership capacity and numbers grew to the point that they could manage the land of their inheritance.

Strange as it may sound, Israel's enemies were less of a threat to their well-being than were the beasts of the field. It's as if God were saying, "I'm going to do you a favor and let the enemy live in your land; it will keep the neighborhood safe." Sometimes, the enemy of my enemy is my friend! In this case, the beasts of the field, left unchecked, would threaten to destroy the crops of the land, and the Canaanites were keeping the beast population at bay. God was like, "If I get rid of your enemy, the beautiful rich farmland will turn into a wasteland."

OVERCOMING THE OBSTACLES OF LIFE IS THE VERY THING THAT PREPARES US FOR OUR DIVINE DESTINY.

WHEN ALL HELL BREAKS LOOSE

Yet there are times when it feels like the enemy of our soul is doing more harm to us than he is to the "beasts of the field"! Have you ever been minding your own business, living a life of comfort and success, when suddenly it feels like the whole world comes crashing down on you? Do you spend a bunch of time trying to figure out what you did wrong, staring at your belly button, hoping some "heavy revy" awakens in your brain and leads you back to the land of tranquility? Well, I certainly have! I found that it's impossible to live a conflictless life and still fulfill our divine purpose. We have to realize that God Himself sometimes leads us into conflict with the enemy to fulfill our divine destiny.

In fact, Jesus is our model for life and ministry. Therefore, it's important to note that Jesus lived on earth for thirty-three years, but we don't know very much about the first thirty years of His life. Then something crazy happened: Jesus was led by the Spirit into the wilderness to be tempted by the devil. Okay, let's think about this: the *Holy Spirit* escorted Jesus into the wilderness for the purpose of being tempted by the devil! Jesus fasted from food and water for forty days as He traversed the desert. On the fortieth day, His weakened body became hungry, and that's when the most profound part of the journey began, because Satan is always attracted to weakness. (See Matthew 4:1–11.)

Just forty short days earlier, Jesus had been baptized by John the Baptist, and an audible voice from heaven had shouted, *"This is my beloved Son, in whom I am well pleased"* (Matthew 3:17). Need I say that this was a "mountaintop" spiritual experience for Jesus? The heavenly Father was so bursting with adoration for His Son that He shouted His affection from heaven to earth, for the whole world to hear! In fact, two thousand years later, His words are still reverberating through history, making massive waves in the sea of humanity.

The devil's accusations cut right to the heart of the weakened state of Christ's humanity. He said, *"If You are the Son of God, command that these stones become bread"* (Matthew 4:3). The question is demeaning and tantalizing: "Are you really...has God really said—or is your personal identity just a messiah complex, a mental disorder, or maybe a bout with narcissism? Perform for your purpose; do something to be someone."

Yet Jesus refused to perform to be a Son because He was already God's Son from eternity; thus His divine birth. His response is epic: *"It is written, 'Man shall not live on bread alone, but on every word that proceeds out of the mouth of God'"* (verse 4). But the devil was not done with his devious devices:

> *Then the devil took Him into the holy city and had Him stand on the pinnacle of the temple, and said to Him, "If You are the Son of God, throw Yourself down; for it is written, 'He will command His angels concerning you'; and 'On their hands they will bear you up, so that you will not strike your foot against a stone.'"* (verses 5–6)

Did you catch that? The enemy tried to get Jesus to commit suicide by using the Word of God against Him! By the way, here Satan quoted

Psalm 91:12, which was actually written about Jesus. The Word of God in the hands of the devil is not truth! The Spirit of God + the Word of God = Truth! The battle raged on as Jesus declared, *"On the other hand, it is written, 'You shall not put the LORD your God to the test'"* (Matthew 4:7).

The devil became increasingly desperate, deciding to throw a Hail Mary:

> *The devil took Him to a very high mountain and showed Him all the kingdoms of the world and their glory; and he said to Him, "All these things I will give You, if You fall down and worship me." Then Jesus said to him, "Go, Satan! For it is written, 'You shall worship the LORD your GOD, and serve Him only.'" Then the devil left Him; and behold, angels came and began to minister to Him.*
>
> (verses 8–11)

The passage about Jesus's temptation in the gospel of Luke concludes like this: *"Jesus returned to Galilee in the power of the Spirit, and news about Him spread through all the surrounding district"* (Luke 4:14). (Read all three gospel accounts of Jesus's conflict with Satan in the wilderness in Matthew 4:1–11, Mark 1:12–13, and Luke 4:1–14.)

A WHOLE NEW ERA

"Kris, why are you telling us this story?" you may probe. That's another great question. We are called to be Christlike, to mirror the Master, to imitate His very life, right? But, as I pointed out earlier, Jesus walked the earth for only thirty-three years, thirty of which we hardly know anything about. So, are we supposed to imitate His entire life or just the last three years of His earthly journey? Well, I believe it's both! I recently realized that Jesus had a sort of "halftime" experience as He came out of the wilderness. He *entered* the wilderness *led by the Spirit* but *exited in the power of the Spirit!* That transition marked a major turning point—*everything changed!*

Let me digress for a minute and give you some insight into where I am going with this. In December 2023, I sought the Lord for a fresh word for the new year. He told me that He wasn't going to give me a prophetic word for 2024; instead, He was giving me a word for a whole new era! The Lord often speaks to us in metaphors and parables that we relate to. True to His nature, the Lord went on to tell me that January 2024 would be the beginning of "halftime," much like an American football game. Halftimes in football aren't just a time to rest but also a time of reflection as the team watches film of the first half of the game to analyze their strategy and make adjustments as necessary. Often, the team that is losing will end up winning the game because of the adjustments they make at halftime. Furthermore, coaches are evaluated by how well they assess problems on the field and adjust their approach to develop winning strategies—especially when they are losing in the first half of the game.

Consequently, the very next weekend after the Lord gave me the halftime word, my favorite team, the San Francisco 49ers, was playing the Detroit Lions for the NFC championship. The 49ers were down by seventeen points at halftime; the score was 24–7. The game was so bad for the 49ers that I turned off the TV and went to work. An hour later, on my way to work, I checked the score, and the 49ers had gone on to win the game. I know it may sound crazy, but I felt like this was a confirming sign from heaven that we are entering a halftime in the Spirit. (Unfortunately, a couple of weeks later, the 49ers were leading in the Super Bowl at halftime, but the Kansas City Chiefs made great halftime adjustments and beat them. Dang! But the principle still held!)

Okay, now let me get back to my main point: for thirty years, Jesus lived sort of under the spiritual radar, and then, after His time in the wilderness, He had a "halftime" experience that catapulted Him into becoming a world changer and a history maker; now, we are following in His footsteps by emerging from under the spiritual radar to fulfill God's world-changing purposes for this time in history. We entered the

COVID-19 season, which was our wilderness period of dealing with the devil. But January 2024 was the beginning of halftime, during which we needed to reassess our game plan, watch some Holy Spirit film, and make adjustments for the new era.

PROPHETIC PROCLAMATION

Thus, I'm going to make a bold proclamation here: we are entering a whole *new era*! Consequently, many of the things that flourished and thrived in the last century, and even in the beginning of the twenty-first century, will become fruitless and futile, requiring pruning and even uprooting—or, to return to our Apollo 11 image, they will require being dropped like boosters that have used up their fuel. Philosopher Eric Hoffer's words ring so relevant to this era: "In times of change, learners inherit the earth, while the learned find themselves beautifully equipped to deal with a world that no longer exists."[24] It's vital that we take this halftime seriously by fortifying our identity (as Jesus did in His duel with the devil in the wilderness), clarifying our purpose, and reimagining our divine opportunities.

IT'S VITAL THAT WE TAKE THIS HALFTIME SERIOUSLY BY FORTIFYING OUR IDENTITY, CLARIFYING OUR PURPOSE, AND REIMAGINING OUR DIVINE OPPORTUNITIES.

Incredible, powerful, and influential doors will be opening to the kingdom of God like never before in modern history. Yet, as someone

24. Eric Hoffer, "Eric Hoffer: Quotes," Goodreads, https://www.goodreads.com/quotes/10562-in-times-of-change-learners-inherit-the-earth-while-the.

once said, "The reason most people do not recognize an opportunity when they meet it is because it usually goes around wearing overalls and looking like Hard Work." Therefore, it's paramount that we keep our spiritual eyes open so that we don't miss a divine opportunity masquerading as a meaningless moment.

To this point, on July 30, 2023, I had a dream about the Lord putting a trumpet to my mouth. He said, "*Blow a trumpet; rally the troops! The kings are coming, the kings are coming! They are coming to help build the kingdom! I am calling for reinforcements.*" I sort of thought I would see some display of obvious royalty in my dream, but the trumpet blast was beckoning fathers and mothers, businesspeople, attorneys, doctors, intercessors, politicians, scientists, technologists, revivalists, and reformers. Educators, builders, and financiers were coming to help extend the borders of the kingdom deep into the cesspools of darkness. "You are called to dirty your hands with the hearts of men," He instructed. Immediately, I saw Isaiah 60:11: "*Your gates will be open continually; they will not be closed day or night, so that men may bring to you the wealth of the nations, with their kings led in procession.*"

I suddenly understood that a new "Jesus movement" was going to grace the entire planet, and kings would be caught up in the procession. In fact, God is joining the prophets, priests, and kings, as He did in the days of Ezra for the rebuilding of Solomon's Temple. On the Friday after I had this encounter, I arranged for a trumpet player to blow a trumpet as a prophetic act of the opening of a new era in all four Sunday morning services at Bethel. But I woke up at 5:00 a.m. on that Sunday with second thoughts and a ton of angst about blowing a trumpet and shouting in church. I was plagued by the idea that the congregation might deem it ridiculous. At 5:05 a.m., I jumped in the tub, fighting off fear as I imagined a trumpet blowing over and over in my mind. At 5:10 a.m., a former Bethel student from the UK named Chris Gaul, whom I hadn't seen or heard from in a decade, sent me a text message. It read, "I felt like I was supposed to send you this Scripture immediately." He had texted me the entire second chapter of Joel, which twice says, "*Blow a trumpet…,"* including in verse 1: *"Blow a trumpet in Zion, and sound an alarm on My holy mountain!"* Consequently, that morning, we blew a trumpet and shouted *"The kings are coming"* in every service! It was so incredibly anointed that the congregation shouted like they were trying to destroy the walls of Jericho.

Are you prepared for this new era?

CONCLUSION: THIS IS OUR MOMENT

Throughout this book, we've journeyed through personal battles and cultural chaos that tempted us to throw in the towel. But here's the call: when everything in you wants to give up, *just stand*. Stand not in your own strength but in the power of the Holy Spirit. He has given you everything you need to triumph over sin and Satan, to be unshakable in the very trials that once threatened to destroy you.

This is our moment. God is preparing us for the era that is emerging. He's not just getting us through—He's raising us up. It's time to embrace the transformation, receive heaven's resources, and walk boldly into the future He's prepared for us.

Let me remind you of what standing looks like:

+ See the caterpillar of your former perspectives and problems undergo a metamorphosis, becoming something new in God's unfolding plan for your life.

+ Drop the encumbrances that are keeping you from moving forward.

+ Recognize your current core values and progressively move toward your high values.

+ Find purpose in suffering and learn to fail successfully.

+ Live from your heavenly position, with a mindset that is future-present, not past-present, reflecting what God says about you and your future.

+ Be yourself and let God's holy attraction draw those around you to Him.

+ Use the supernatural gifts of His superior kingdom to wage warfare against the enemy.

+ Model both the compassion and the zeal of Jesus.

+ Instead of running from conflict, allow it to bring out the greatness God has put within you.

+ Use this "halftime" season to prepare for a new era of kingdom power and fruitfulness.

Culturally, the bad news is that we are in an intense battle for the very soul of our planet, like no other time in modern history. The family unit is failing, as we live in one of the most fatherless generations in history, where our fathers are alive but not home.[25] As a matter of fact, about 40 percent of all children in America are born out of wedlock, many of them living without their dads.[26] Beyond that enormous problem, suicide has become a pandemic, being one of the leading causes of death in the United States, affecting people of all ages, genders, social classes, and ethnic groups.[27] The LGBTQ+ movement has infiltrated every sphere of society, threatening the very core of our identity and putting the youngest of our flock in grave danger—negatively shaping their thinking, their choices, and, ultimately, the way they live. Men claiming to be women invade our girls' locker rooms and restrooms. They compete against women in sports, usurp their trophies, and undermine their scholarships! In recent years, governmental institutions—particularly

25. Joseph Chamie, "America's Single-Parent Households and Missing Fathers," NIUSSP, January 13, 2025, https://www.niussp.org/family-and-households/americas-single-parent-households-and-missing-fathers/.
26. "Unmarried Childbearing," FastStats, National Center for Health Statistics, Centers for Disease Control and Prevention (CDC), https://www.cdc.gov/nchs/fastats/unmarried-childbearing.htm; "Percentage of Births to Unmarried Women in the United States from 1980 to 2023," Statista, https://www.statista.com/statistics/276025/us-percentage-of-births-to-unmarried-women/.
27. "Suicide Prevention," US Centers for Disease Control and Prevention, March 26, 2025, https://www.cdc.gov/suicide/facts/data.html.

in states like California—have played an increasingly direct role in decisions around gender identity for minors.[28] In certain situations, especially when children enter the foster care system or are in contested custody cases, medical and psychological transitions may proceed without the full knowledge or consent of both parents.[29] Parents who do not affirm their child's perceived transgender identity have been called "abusive." There have been cases where various child protective services have removed children from their homes and placed them in a transgender-friendly foster care system.[30] I could go on and on, but, needless to say, the situation has become dire!

But the good news is, we are in a new era, and God is on the move. We are literally living in the tipping point of history. In fact, allow me to be so bold as to say that *we* are the tipping point of history! We entered this wilderness led by the Spirit to be tempted by the devil—not so that he can beat us, but so that we can annihilate his devious, deceptive, and destructive plot. Now we are about to exit the wilderness in the power of the Spirit. Just like during Jesus's thirty years of relative silence before He emerged to defeat Satan, the devil hasn't yet felt the full force of our divine purpose, but we are about to emerge with a vengeance. As the great prophet and teacher Lisa Bevere points out in her book *The Fight for Female,* "God...put enmity between the serpent and the woman." Lisa explains that, because of this, we—the seed of the woman (see Genesis 3:15)—don't have irreconcilable differences with the devil,

28. "Education Code–EDC," California Legislative Information," https://leginfo.legislature.ca.gov/faces/codes_displaySection. xhtml?sectionNum=220.3.&nodeTreePath=1.1.1.2.6&lawCode=EDC.

29. Abigail Shrier, "Child Custody's Gender Gauntlet," *City Journal,* Manhattan Institute, February 7, 2022, https://www.city-journal.org/article/child-custodys-gender-gauntlet; Jackson Walker, "'Framed as a Bigot': NY Father Loses Custody of Son After Questioning Gender Transition," February 5, 2024, https://nbcmontana.com/news/nation-world/ framed-as-a-bigot-ny-father-loses-custody-of-son-after-questioning-gender-transition- software-engineer-dennis-hannon-32-told-the-national-desk-tnd-monday-the-erie-county- supreme-court-upstate-new-york-transgender-lgbtq-rights-trans.

30. Ashley Vaughan, "State Shouldn't Seize Children from Parents over Differing Gender Views," *The Carolina Journal,* May 8, 2025, https://www.carolinajournal.com/opinion/state- shouldnt-seize-children-from-parents-over-differing-gender-views/.

we have "irreconcilable hostility" toward him![31] The bride of Christ is inherently hostile toward the devil. In fact, an inner hatred toward him is seething below the surface of our lives that finds great pleasure in destroying the works of the devil.

WE ARE ABOUT TO EXIT THE WILDERNESS IN THE POWER OF THE SPIRIT.

Furthermore, there is a call for a divine union that is already growing in the Spirit and that is attracting the prophets, priests, and kings toward a common cause—the discipling of the nations—while experiencing the kingdoms of this world become the kingdom of our God. (See Revelation 11:15.) I love the prophet Daniel's insights into the end-time ministry of the saints. Six hundred years before Christ, he prophesied:

> *The court will sit for judgment, and his [Satan's] dominion will be taken away, annihilated and destroyed forever. Then the sovereignty, the dominion and the greatness of all the kingdoms under the whole heaven will be given to the people of the saints of the Highest One; His kingdom will be an everlasting kingdom, and all the dominions will serve and obey Him.* (Daniel 7:26–27)

The devil fears you to the core of his being. He's deeply concerned that you are going to discover *whose* you are and *who* you are, and thus reconcile your life with your divine purpose, your radical call, and your supernatural power. While much of the world has gone *woke*, the Lord is kissing His bride *awake*, just in time to experience the full power and protection of the Bridegroom! It's time to wake up because salvation is

---

31. Lisa Bevere, *The Fight for Female: Reclaiming Our Divine Identity* (Grand Rapids, MI: Revell, 2024), 11.

nearer than you might think! The night is slipping away, so dress your-self in *"the armor of light"* (see Romans 13:11–12) and enter *"the womb of the dawn"* (Psalm 110:3) of a whole new era.

ABOUT THE AUTHOR

Kris Vallotton is an author, an international speaker, a cultural leader, and, most of all, a spiritual father to this generation. As Senior Associate Leader of Bethel Church in Redding, California, and the cofounder of Bethel School of Supernatural Ministry (BSSM) and Moral Revolution, Kris has helped thousands of believers over the past twenty years to realize their identity as sons and daughters of God. He's a best-selling author, having written more than a sixteen books and training manuals to help prepare believers for life in the kingdom.

Kris has a diverse background in business, counseling, consulting, pastoring, and teaching, which gives him unique leadership insights and perspectives. He's a highly-sought-after international speaker, equipping people to successfully fulfill their divine purpose. Kris loves to both teach the masses and advise leaders one-on-one, utilizing his experience and his prophetic gift to assist world influencers in achieving their goals. He commonly provides counsel to governmental and business leaders on practical strategies for cultural transformation, and he has unique expertise in economies and building prosperous communities.

Though Kris is renowned for his writing and speaking, he and his wife of fifty years, Kathy, are also successful entrepreneurs who co-owned nine businesses in the automotive industry. Kris is the founder of the Bethel School of Technology, the chairman of Advance Redding, and the founder of Bethel Media.

Kris and Kathy live in beautiful Redding, California, with their dog, Samson, and Kathy's horses, Bailey and Legend. When he's home, you can find him playing basketball, working on his small ranch, or building furniture in his workshop. You can also find him watching Kathy ride her horses, as he is not a full-blown cowboy himself (yet).